THE MARYS OF
MEDIEVAL DRAMA

Sidestone Press

THE MARYS OF MEDIEVAL DRAMA

THE MIDDLE ENGLISH DIGBY AND N-TOWN IN TRANSLATION

Colleen E. Donnelly

© 2016 C.E. Donnelly

Published by Sidestone Press, Leiden
www.sidestone.com

ISBN 978-90-8890-367-0

Lay-out & cover design: Sidestone Press

Photograph cover: "The Visitation", from "Psalter (The 'Melisende Psalter') with
canticles, prayers, and litany". Coll. British Library, Egerton 1139 f. 1v

Also available as:
PDF e-book ISBN 978-90-8890-368-7

Contents

For Robert Mines

who always believes

Introduction

Mary Magdalene and the Virgin Mary continue to intrigue and fascinate us to this day. Their biblical interludes are brief, piquing our curiosity and compelling speculation about the unknown years of their lives. *The Last Temptation of Christ*, Dan Brown's *DaVinci Code*, and Kathleen McGowan's *Magdalene Line* are just a few of the more recent works that demonstrate that we are enthralled with Mary Magdalene's story to this day—sparking conjecture about her relationship with Christ and prompted by a desire to know more about the life of the woman known as the model penitent. Well within recent memory, two popes, John Paul and Benedict have had to address the more than millennium enduring misnomer that Mary Magdalene was a prostitute—a confusion started by Pope Gregory in a homily in 591, which conflating the prostitute that anointed Christ's feet in Luke 7:36-48 with Mary Magdalene from whom Christ exorcised demons in Luke 8:2 and Mary of Bethany of John 11:1-2. Early gnostic materials give her a more prevalent role as disciple of Christ, in the company of the apostles as he teaches them, and one of a chosen few presented as asking him questions. Legend attributes the conversion of France, specifically through Marseilles, to her. The thirst for more information, for a more comprehensive hagiography, saint's life, of this revered and emulated woman, known through only a few verses of the New Testament, should not surprise us. The centuries of stories surrounding her not only offer a window into how she was perceived throughout history, but her reception also reflects how religious women were perceived by their own society in their day.

The Virgin Mary occupies an interesting role in religious history. Attacking the Catholic adoration of the Virgin Mary, Protestants minimalize her role,[1] disavow the Assumption, and change the Annunciation by Gabriel from "Hail Mary, full of grace," which connotes born without sin, to "Hail, thou art highly favored" (Luke 1:28) to minimalize the unique purity and piety she possessed. For Catholics, she is not only the mother of God, through whom the redemption story begins; like Mary Magdalene, she is another female role model of humility and piety. The Virgin is capable of interceding on behalf of man, who humbled by his flawed humanity, seeks her assistance in beseeching the divine God. Beginning in the first centuries of Christianity, additional stories about her birth and youth can be found that were circulated and sustained outside the canonical gospels of the New Testament; these delve into the conduct and demeanor that won her God's preferment, shining a light on the nature of her betrothal and chaste marriage to Joseph, as well as addressing the skepticism about her condition likely voiced by the Jewish community. As with Mary Magdalene, these stories that add more to

---

1   Much of the non-liturgical Mary material that disappeared in the vernacular in later centuries can, in part, be attributed to the Protestant reformation's rejection of the veneration of Mary which they perceived as idolatry. In response, the Catholic Church may have also tightened its control on her image.

our understanding of this woman who we get only glimpses of in Scripture, may offer us insight into how common Catholics viewed and related to her throughout history, as well as to how her image shaped roles for women in the Church.

Women in Early Christianity and the Middle Ages

The images of these women are important in considering a response to the long standing antifeminist tradition of the Church which dates back to St. Paul, the male apostolic tradition, and which was strengthened by a patriarchal hierarchy that blamed Eve for the Fall of Man and denied women positions of influence in its institution. We know that women played an important role in the conversion to Christianity in the first centuries. Upper class women materially supported the apostles, providing them with food, clothing, and by inviting the disciples into their homes. Various Christian groups met in homes rather than churches, spreading Christianity through households and communities. Historians of early Christianity argue that the majority of Christians in the first century were women.[2] The marriage of an aristocratic Catholic woman could lead to the conversion of her husband, followed by his household. Many brides demanded the freedom to practice their religion and to bring priests with them, which lead to the spread of the faith throughout the community. If her husband were a lord of significant status, this could be an important impetus for the conversion of the pagan territory.

In the centuries that followed, passionately devout women could chose to serve God in an contemplative environment that offered an alternative to the secular life of wife and mother. A monastic life within an exclusively female community was a credible choice for a woman in the Middle Ages.[3] The lifetime devotion to this calling also afforded some women an opportunity for education, leading to the production of renown writing of many female spiritual writers, such as Hroswitha, Julian of Norwich, and Hildegard of Bingen.

In the latter part of the Middle Ages (1300-1500), art, documents, and recorded events give us a very interesting view of how women were perceived within the Church and how they engaged their religion, countering an often modern notion of a solely misogynistic Church oppressing the female members of its constituency. This period saw unprecedented opportunities for women practicing their piety. Historically, it is an apex of female religious life and veneration. In 1405, Christine de Pizan addressed the antifeminist tradition in part one of *The Book of the City of Ladies* writing that God only creates good, and, since God created woman, woman must be good (I.1.2). Between 1200-1500, over one hundred women were added to the rolls of saints, far more than in any previous period. The number of convents and nunneries exponentially increased, and the influence of women was more profoundly felt within the Church. New orders of nuns and laywomen serving God arose, from the Brigittines to the Beguines (who like the Lollards

---

2   See for example, Rodney Stark, *The Rise of Christianity*, (San Francisco: Harper, 1996).

3   The Protestant Church disavowed a woman's right to pursue a contemplative, religious life, available to Catholic women in the Middle Ages. Both Luther and Calvin decreed that women belonged in the home, and there, the good protestant woman stayed. The King James Bible actually erases the Old Testament stories of Susanna and Judith and deletes more than six chapters of the Book of Ester found in the Catholic Douay-Rheims Bible, relegating this material to Apocrypha.

questioned the authority of male preaching and the limits on the roles of the laity) and Cathars who emulated Mary Magdalene as an important teacher and leader in the early Church. Leading churchwomen, particularly abbesses, gained power rivaling queens, and otherwise not available to women in the Middle Ages, treating with kings, bishops, and even popes. Bridget of Sweden made a pilgrimage to the Pope to establish her house and order. Catherine of Sienna consulted papal legates and negotiated for the city states of Italy; she counseled for reform of the clergy and was influential in convincing Pope Gregory XI to leave Avignon, where the Holy See had moved in 1307, and has been considered one of the voices influential in restoring it to Rome.[4] Female spiritual writing and mysticism flourished during the late Middle Ages; Hildegard of Bingen, Julian of Norwich, Bridget of Sweden, Mechthild of Magdeburg, Hadewijch of Antwerp, Teresa of Avila and others wrote works for the clergy and laity. The Cult of Tears,[5] the Cult of the Virgin, the veneration of Our Lady of Sorrows, and most significantly the legacy of the modern rosary all began during this period. This is not to say that women held positions of power or participated in determining and directing policy, but women were not simply dismissed as daughters of Eve who were to graciously endure either indifference or abuse from the Church until delivered to their heavenly reward. Rather, female sanctity and devotion were more commonly practiced and celebrated than ever before and inroads were made in including women in the redemptive history of mankind.

The Reputation of the Virgin Mary and Mary Magdalene in the Middle Ages

Not surprisingly, these increased opportunities were accompanied by a flowering of female images in art and literature that encouraged devotion and offered models for behavior. Many orders of nuns, female mystics, and laywomen clearly looked for images and role models by which to model their own lives. Aristocratic women also commissioned hagiographies for their devotional practices.

The Virgin Mary and Mary Magdalene were most revered. The Venerations of the Virgin Mary and Mary Magdalene were endorsed by such respected authorities as Duns Scotus, Bernard of Clarivox, Thomas Aquinas, and Peter Abelard. Abelard wrote that tears shed by a women had the power to intercede for man and sway God, a tradition predicated on the tears wept by the Virgin and the Magdalene at the Passion. During the Middle Ages, the veneration of the Virgin Mary dramatically increased. Numerous miracles associated with her were recorded in both Latin and the vernacular languages in the twelfth and thirteenth century. Mariology contributed to the rise of chivalry and played a major role in defining the role of the female Christian and inspiring women choosing the contemplative life of

---

4   During Babylonian Captivity, the Papal See was moved to Avignon France under a French pope (1307-1377); following sustained subsequent challenges, the papal court returned to Rome. The Great Schism ensued until 1417, during which time there was a pope in France and one in Rome. Since there can only be one pope who is the voice of God on earth, this caused great unrest and damage to the Church at that time.

5   Note that the term "cult" denotes devotion or veneration. In the Middle Ages, it does not connote a dangerous fringe movement.

religious houses. In fact, the Holy House in Walsingham in England was erected in the late twelfth century, as a replica of the house in which the Annunciation took place, and became a royally sponsored, major pilgrimage site. The tradition of Mary as intercessor was well establish in popular piety in the Late Middle Ages; "The Hours of the Blessed Virgin Mary" was recited in English churches in the later half of the fourteenth century. In East Anglia, the most populated area of England at the time, Mariology and a tradition of female piety were well established and practiced:

> *"Late medieval East Anglia lays claim to more anchoresses and female recluses and a created concentration of female religious houses than any other area in England. It was home to the only known medieval English female mystics and a vital center of the insular Cults of the Virgin Mary and her mother St. Anne. In the 15th century, it emerges as an unacknowledged hub for the production of texts linked to female devotion and female construction of the sacred"* (Coletti 46).[6]

In England, while only two churches were dedicated to Mary Magdalene in 1100, at the close of the Middle Ages there were close to two hundred, attesting to the rise in popularity of the veneration of the Magdalene. But what exactly were the images of these two women, what was known of the mother of God, capable of interceding for man, and Mary Magdalene the repentant sinner, available not only for women called to religious orders but also to lay women, inspiring their devotion?

Vernacular Religion

In addressing that question, we must acquaint ourselves with a few important facts of that time. During this period, 1300-1500, over ninety-five percent of the population was illiterate and could not read. Moreover, there was no Bible in the vernacular, ordinary English language; the only Bible was in Latin. The first complete English New Testament was not available until 1526, translated by William Tyndale, and the complete English Bible, translated by Myles Coverdale, appeared in 1535. The printing press was invented in 1450, in Germany. Until the printing press became commonly used to published texts throughout Europe in the next century, all Bibles and the far more numerous sections of it that were excerpted, prayer books, hymnals, bestiaries, and all other religious materials had to be copied by hand. A majority of the religious written texts were held by the Church, especially by the larger and better endowed monasteries, abbeys, and universities. (Many universities were started and supported by the Church, if not by the crown.) This means that religion and faith were experienced by most of the population in two ways, visually and aurally. Given that the Mass was performed in Latin, beyond Mass, the visual art and spectacle and the storytelling components of the Catholic faith were integral to lay practitioners experience of their faith. Plays started in the churches developing out of processions and church pageantry, but in 1210 Pope Innocent the III banned priests' participation in these dramas. This

---

6   Theresa Coletti, *Mary Magdalene And The Drama Of Saints: Theater, Gender, And Religion In Late Medieval England*, (Philadelphia: University of Pennsylvania Press) 2004.

resulted in the plays moving to the streets and being performed by laymen and developing into the rich tradition of medieval biblical-based drama. They became the property of the laity and took on the qualities of vernacular religion—cultural performances reflecting common beliefs and attitudes toward religious materials held by the general populace. During this period, the calendar was filled with religious observances and feast days that were celebrated in this way. *The Digby Mary Magdalene* likely began to honor the saint's feast day. It may be interesting to note, as attested to by the popularity of the cycle plays in England, that the Catholic Church did not interfere with the performances, perhaps accepting them as a viable way of disseminating religious material, though they would later banned by a protestant government. The plays of the Magdalene and the Virgin May also testify to the effort made in late medieval vernacular religious culture to address women as consumers of religious texts and experience.

Middle English Biblically Based Drama

The popularity of these plays, particularly in the English tradition and language, is attested to by a number of factors. Authors from Chaucer to Shakespeare allude to their performance. We have records of the performance of Biblical cycle plays in a number of cities during the fourteenth and fifteenth century, and a number of cycles are named after the area in which they were performed (Chester, York, Towneley and Coventry). We do not know who penned the plays, and the texts we have likely underwent numerous modifications and emendations throughout the years. We call these plays "cycle plays" because they contain ten to fifty individual plays that include important events from the Bible such as the Creation, Noah's Flood, the Nativity, the Passion, and the Last Judgment. Different cycles from different towns include different Old and New Testament stories, though all include the Passion and Resurrection. Each play probably took five to fifteen minutes to perform. They were often performed over the day or a few days at a number of stations or intersections throughout the city and often on pageant wagons. Each wagon, resembling the modern parade float, was one "story" that would move to various intersections of the city and be performed throughout the day(s). Play one, the Creation, would be performed at station one, then proceeded to intersection two to be performed again, while play two, the Fall of Man, was performed by the second wagon company in intersection one, and so on. Audiences would gather and watch, and most likely interact with the performers. (The idea of silently watching a play on a stage is a more modern notion.)

The *N-Town Cycle* was probably not performed on pageant wagons, though the plays were probably performed in small outside staging areas. The *N-Town Cycle* is most likely a compilation of plays from various playwrights and locales. There was no single writer, plays were added, and the cycle was revised a number of times from the late fourteenth into the early fifteenth century. "N" stands in for the city where the plays were performed; hence when plays were performed in Newgate, they would be known as the Newgate Cycle. Unlike the other cycles—*York*, *Chester* and *Towneley*—the *N-Town* was probably never performed in its entirety. The *N-Town* collection was likely a library of plays that could be borrowed and performed, lent out and copied for production, whereas other cycles were performed by local trade and craft guilds that took responsibility for their production.

The Mary Play, which is a recognized part of the *N-Town Cycle,* includes Marian materials not found in other cycles: "Joachim and Anne," "The Presentation of Mary in the Temple," "The Trial of Mary and Joseph," and "The Visit to Elizabeth." "The Assumption" was a later addition to the cycle, demonstrating language features of a different author, and requiring a much larger cast and more elaborate staging. I have added additional *N-Town* plays concerning Mary to complete the story of the life of Mary as found in this cycle, and call it the *Mary Plays.* As plays were added, and materials were revised and required more elaborate sets, performances may have moved to a set staging area, like the longer, miracle and conversion plays which consisted of multiple scenes and requiring multiple sets, such as the *Digby Mary Magdalene.*

Another type of performance also developed during the fifteenth century, the morality play. These plays represented the common man's entire life and followed his or her fall into vice and subsequent road to redemption and salvation, modeling Christian behavior for the audience. These plays more greatly resemble the modern plays with which we are familiar. Many of the plays are about individuals beset by allegorical figures depicting sin—pride, wrath, and sloth—and depict the sinner's road back to God. *The Digby Mary Magdalene* is a saint's life or conversion play. Unlike these morality plays, it was intended to be performed on a circular stage, with a center area, called "the Place," where the major action occurred, with small scaffolds or stages on the circumference representing other areas such as hell, a landing dock, and the courts of various Roman officials. This resembles our modern theater in the round. Rather than the depiction of a typical person or "everyman" hero like the morality play, the *Digby Magdalene* is about a known saint. There are a number of saint's life/conversion plays that survive from this period; they are most often a dramatic rendering of a hagiography, incorporating both what would be considered orthodox historic and fantastic legendary material about the saint and including the conversion of pagans to the right faith, thus teaching the same message as the morality play, but depicted through the idealized life of a saint and the conversion of others rather than the return to faith and redemption of the common man.

In all cases, the plays were a significant venue for Catholics to learn and experience their religion. What is interesting for us is how these plays represented the Marys, what was added to orthodox Scripture, what was constructed for and by contemporary society that offers us an insight into their vision of these venerable Christian women.

Why these plays and what are their origins?

These plays offer us an opportunity to examine how communities in an earlier era engaged and experienced their religion. Clearly Latin theological texts were relatively unknown to the laity, and the oral history and storytelling that these people participated in is lost to us today. These plays, then, are some of the few surviving artifacts recording how Biblical materials were available to lay people in the vernacular, English. They provide a link between apocryphal and gnostic materials from the first four centuries of Christianity, that were denounced, destroyed and supposedly eradicated by the Church, but which clearly survived secreted or in oral tradition, passed down for over a thousand years, influencing contemporary medieval religious belief and practices. We know during the early centuries of Christianity the gospels were spread primarily by being preached orally; heard rather than read, they spread aurally. Today, we know about many of these non-canonical texts from discovered and recovered manuscripts, such at those of the *Nag Hammadi* Scriptures, as well as by tracing the history and transmission of Biblical and Christian-based material, as we are pursuing here. There is yet another fascinating fact to consider. The earliest surviving versions of these suppressed texts were written in Greek, and later, after the fourth or fifth century, in Latin. The plays included here are in English. This suggests that while written texts were suppressed, these stories so captured the imagination and hearts of people that they were retold in the common, vernacular languages of Europe, crossing geographical boundaries, and were passed down orally for over a millennium. Legendary materials that developed over the ensuing centuries, and elements that gave the plays a contemporary flair—such as identifiably medieval midwives, sailors, and soldiers—were used to embellished and elaborated scriptural sources. Still an abundant amount of the source material of these plays can be traced back to texts written during the early centuries of Christianity.

The Mary Plays[7] owe much to the tradition begun by *The Infancy Gospel of James,* likely written in the mid second century A.D., which contains some of the earliest episodes of Mary's childhood, including her presentation in the temple, the choice of Joseph as her spouse and subsequent marriage, and the trial by ordeal that they are forced to endure when her pregnancy becomes evident. Perhaps the most interesting additions to the more orthodox gospels of the New Testament center on the very natural, human apprehension and skepticism that the announcement of the virginal conception certain would have evoked. This topic is visited in the *Gospel of James,* as Jewish priests and rabbis, midwives, and Joseph question the miracle. While Joseph's doubt is briefly addressed in Matthew 1:19-20, it receives much greater treatment in the *Gospel of James*, where Joseph also voices his concern that Mary could be condemned to death for adultery. After Jesus's birth, midwives who examine Mary authoritatively attest to her intact virginity and put any remaining doubts to rest. Materials used for the "The Assumption" play can be traced back to "The Account of St. John the Theologian of the Falling Asleep of the Holy Mother of God," most likely composed in the early seventh century, and the first and second Latin form of the "Passing of Mary" which were probably composed in the fourth century A.D. Apocrypha stories of Christ visiting his mother before arising from the tomb go back to a potential misread of St. Ambrose's *de Virginitate* (late fourth century) and were part of contemporary culture in the late Middle Ages. Margery Kempe speaks of Christ's appearance to his mother in a vision in her dictated autobiography, and Teresa of Avila also writes about such a visit; the

---

7   Though not considered part of the *N-Town Mary Play*, as essential to the Marion material, I have included "Joseph's Doubt," "The Purification," Christ's "Appearance to Mary," and "The Assumption of Mary," and for this reason refer to my translation as the *Mary Plays*.

tradition was affirmed and embraced by many medieval theologians, beginning with St Anselm (ca. 1100).

The Digby Mary Magdalene is an interesting composite, drawing from a large number of Biblical, apocryphal, and legendary sources. Karen L. King has traced a number of oral versions of Mary Magdalene's life back to the second century, when the gospels were most commonly verbally spread by preachers to attentive audiences.[8] In the play, Mary is not only the exemplary penitent sinner, she is the apostle to the apostles, and, like the male apostles, she converts pagans to Christianity; her story is a hagiography, and her elevation to saint and apostle is enhanced by her comparison to the Virgin Mary, which was common in the veneration of Mary Magdalene in the late Middle Ages. This play can be confusing because it is not always linear, jumping through Biblical and historic time and geographical space. The intent is to universalize the message of the redemption of the penitent sinner by utilizing various canonical and non-Scriptural materials spoken and penned about the Magdalene and passed down through the centuries. Central to the development of her character is Gregory's composite Mary, the prostitute who washed Jesus' feet at Simeon's house (Luke 737-50), the woman from whom Jesus exorcised demons and one of the women who supported and traveled with the apostles (Luke 8:1-3), and Mary of Bethany, sister of Lazarus and Martha (John 11:1-2). The play clearly uses orthodox materials from the Bible, invoking Luke 8:2, and making the "seven devils" driven from her the seven deadly sins. The tradition of female exorcism associated with Mary Magdalene dates back to Gregory the Great. In addition, both scriptural versions of Christ's appearance to her at his tomb are included in the play: in one, he appears to her alone (John 20:1); in the other, he appears to her in the company of Mary mother of James, and Mary Salome, who all come to anoint his body.

The tradition of Mary as a chosen apostle, and apostles to the apostles, derives from many gnostic texts of the second through the fourth century, including the *Gospels of Mary, Philip,* and *Thomas,* the *Dialogue of the Savior,* and *Pistis Sophia.* Mary is numbered among the apostles taught by Christ, specifically named, sometimes singled out by being mentioned by name in the text or addressed by Christ, and is one of the few allowed to directly ask him questions. She is a central figure in Gnosticism which concentrates more on the "secret," special knowledge and teaching of Christ as the road to redemption rather than the resurrection. This is not to say that these written texts were available and read in the Middle Ages, but rather that the gnostic tradition establishing Mary as a favored disciple of Christ definitely survived. In the early ninth century, Rabanus Maurus in his *Life of Mary Magdalene,* not only called her an apostles, but also named her as the apostle to the apostles, harkening back to the gnostic tradition of the first centuries.

Odo of Cluny, a 10th century Benedictine monk, is credited with characterizing her family as nobility, and in Jacobus de Voragine's *Legenda Aurea* (*The Golden Legend*), they become royalty, ruling and controlling property. Many other texts written in the Late Middle Ages besides the *Digby Mary Magdalene* likely derived from Voragine's *Legenda Aurea,* such as John Mirk's "Sermon on St. Mary

---

8   Karen L. King, *The Gospel of Mary of Magdala: Jesus and the First Woman Apostle* (Polebridge: Salem, 2003) 94.

Magdalene" and her story in the *South English Legendary*. *The Legendary* circulated among medieval audiences and was also likely known by the writer of the *Digby Mary Magdalene*.

Voragine's *Legenda Aurea* was one of the most popular books circulating in the late Middle Ages, first published in Latin ca. 1275. William Caxton first translated and printed it into English in 1483; nine editions were published over the next fifty years. This text appears to be the most direct source of the story of Mary's life after Pentecost. Like the male apostles, she is said to have embarked on a mission to covert pagans; her mission is to Marseilles. Following her success, she withdraws from society to live the life of an ascetic devoted to God, and readers are treated to details of her death and internment. Voragine most likely drew from earlier French legends that claim she converted Provence; the mythical conversion of Gaul, a large region of what was later to become France, is attributed to Mary, and her brother Lazarus and sister Martha. The Provencal oral tradition also included Lazarus becoming the first Bishop of Marseilles. In the French legends of the preceding centuries that influenced Voragine's work, Mary lived for thirty years in the wilderness, died, and was buried in Saint-Maximin-la-Sainte-Baume, Provence. In English, evidence of the tradition of her later life as a hermit is found as early as 900 A.D., in the *Old English Martyrology*. Medieval accounts of her hermetic later years and her death appear to incorporate elements of Greek legend of the reformed prostitute St. Mary of Egypt (from the ninth century). There may have been cross-contamination and confusion of Mary of Egypt and Mary Magdalene stories, resembling the conflation of scriptural episodes concerning the Magdalene.

The Cult of the Magdalene swelled, following the purported discovery of the sarcophagi containing her remains beneath the Church of St. Maximum in 1279; upon that discover, Charles d'Anjou erected the Basilica in her honor on the site. Illuminating the life of the model penitent, witness to Christ in life and death, sent forth to spread His message, and later living as an ascetic, Mary Magdalene's story resonates with scripture and theological tradition, as well as contemporary spiritual ideas and practices. Her story may well have inspired religious and lay women in their daily devotions and lent authority to their engagement in female piety.

Historical and Contemporary Issues

Most of the writing of the Middle Ages was done anonymously. A commonly held belief, particularly in reference to religious writing which dominated the period, was that God was the sole author. The writer was simply the instrument through which God wrote; therefore, the human tool, or writer, seldom signed his work. An author in this age was primarily a compilator and/or translator, taking older materials and making their messages accessible to the contemporary public, giving those materials a contemporary guise. Medieval writers commonly combined Scriptural and legendary materials with clearly contemporary aspects of their own world. We do not know who wrote the *Digby Mary Magdalene*. The author clearly knew the *Golden Legend* and other contemporary sources that draw from the long tradition of the Magdalene story identified here, and he added a few humorous and entertaining contemporary elements such at the banter and slapstick between the boat captain and the crew-hand and the priest and boy in the temple of Mohammed. An author's ability to use techniques that made the material more entertaining and memorable, as well as the audience's familiarity with certain liturgical, Biblical, and legendary elements and devices, may have played a large part in determining what was penned and performed at the time. Elements that offended, appeared heretical, or that seemed insignificant or poorly rendered were most likely not preserved for posterity.

We must also recognize that medieval people did not have our knowledge of linear history and chronology, nor did they worry about anachronisms such as Biblical Roman rulers and soldiers behaving like medieval feudal rulers and knights. They believed that the messages of Christian history were repeated in different ages, and the goal was always to convey and understand the message. Through allegory, a literal current event or image could resonant and evoke a Biblical one or a doctrinal message; an advisor who commits treason against his king, such as Brutus against Caesar, is comparable to Judas' betraying his Lord.[9] In the *Mary Plays*, the medieval theologian would recognize the literal blooming of Joseph's branch in "The Marriage" as corresponding typologically to the blooming of Aaron's rod in Numbers 17 or Moses and the burning bush (the bush not being consumed is seen as prefiguring the virgin birth), as tropologically evoking Mary as the barren virgin who "blooms" without male seed, and anagogically, as bringing eternal salvation of the world through the birth of Christ.

The most common anachronism is the invocation of the Trinity, which is found in many of the Jewish temple scenes in the *Mary Plays* (for example, in "The Presentation of Mary" lines 23, 74, and 301). Jewish characters often recite verses or allude to events found in the New Testament. Some issues of Judaic law take on medieval Christian attributes: Joachim's Judaic expulsion from the temple would be seen by contemporary society as Catholic excommunication. In addition, medieval audiences would have recognized facets of the Mass in the temple scenes. The reason for this is familiar to medieval and modern Christians alike: the Old Testament is being rendered as the prequel for the New Testament; figures and events conspire to create the conditions necessary to fulfill the promise of the coming Messiah, to bring about the New Law foreseen in the Old Testament.

The Mary Plays impressively render some Judaic customs and laws, as in the manner in which Ysakar tests Mary piety and maturity in having her recite the Gradual Psalms for the fifteen steps between the courts of men and women from the Gate of Nicanor to Herod's Temple in "The Presentation of Mary," and the mandate on the marriage of pubescent girls. Mosaic laws governing the punishment for adultery (as recorded in Leviticus 20:10, Deuteronomy 22:22) and the story of

---

9   Allegory was a manner of reading that illuminated the four levels of meaning that can be found in liturgical texts: 1) The Literal (historical, Old Testament, or individual)—what the story actually says; 2) Typological (allegorical, New Testament, type or group)—illustrates truths; 3) Moral (tropological)—the conversion of soul, what should be done; 4) Anagogical (eschatological)—deals with "the four last things"—Death, Judgment, Heaven and Hell—or eternity. For example, Moses would be 2) Jesus, 3) the savior and the way, 4) eternal salvation.

the female adulterer in Numbers 5:11-31 fuel Joseph's fears about Mary's fate in "Joseph's Doubt" and the "Trial of Mary and Joseph." The presentation of Joseph as a humiliated cuckold is distinctively medieval. "The Trial" is an interesting refiguring of Mosaic Law in terms of the New Law. Trial by ordeal, intended to prove whether the accused was being truthful, was actually conducted in the Late Middle Ages. Judaic law and custom is treated respectfully in the early *Mary Plays*. This is interesting considering anti-Semitism was strong in England: the Jews were expelled from England at the end of the thirteenth century, and they were often blamed for the epidemic of Bubonic Plague. In the "Assumption Play," the Jews merge with the "so-called pagan" followers of Mohammad, and become the infidels and enemies of Christian medieval Europe and the Crusades. The enemy is often treated with disdain or abused, as well as humiliated through humor that depicts the infidel as imbecile, while providing comic interludes for the audience. This is evident in "The Assumption Play," when one of the Jewish priests attacks Mary's body and in the verbal banter between the priest and the boy in Mohammed's temple the *Digby Mary Magdalene*.

The plays are also a record of both medieval theological practice and debate. While Mariology flourished in the Late Middle Ages, so did discussion and debate about the Virgin Mother. During the later part of the Middle Ages, the idea of Mary as a second Eve, without original sin and incorrupt, and playing a part in the redemptive history becomes popular, championed by the fathers of the Church beginning with Bernard of Clairvaux (ca. 1100). The idea that Mary was free from sin had been established many centuries earlier, but the notion of her being conceived without original sin, as reflected in "Joachim and Anne" and "The Trial of Mary and Joseph," became more widespread after the writings of Duns Scotus, ca. 1300. The issue was resolved by the Council of Basel, in 1439, and confirmed by the celebration of the Feast of the Immaculate Conception, in 1482 (and again proclaimed by Pius IX, in the *Constitution Ineffabilis Deus*, in 1894). The fourteenth century witnessed debate as to whether Mary's body ascended with her or her soul ascended after Christ sent her back to reclaim her body for assumption (dormition); this is reflected in the "Assumption" play which draws from the gnostic tradition of dormition, while the prevailing orthodox belief dictates that her body and soul were assumed together. By the mid-fifteenth century, the redemption story was commonly seen as not beginning with the Annunciation but with the story of Mary's conception. The veneration of Mary added a maternal, nurturing element to Catholicism, and, particularly in the "Nativity" and "Assumption," we see her interceding for man: when wrong belief is revealed and punished, those guided by her direction and assisted by her intervention are then cured and find salvation. During the Middle Ages, miracles were continually attributed to Mary; the plays help to commemorate a history of the miracles that began during her lifetime and which were a testament to her legacy.

The Digby Mary Magdalene also reflects theological debates of the time. Central to the *Digby* play is the issue of the role of woman in the Church, particularly in regard to teaching and preaching. During the late fourteenth and early fifteen century, this question originally brought up by Paul (Tim 2:11-12 and 1 Cor 14:34-35) took center stage once again, and Lollardry, a precursor to Protestantism that challenged papal authority and the Church hierarchy, argued that women could preach. (In "The Assumption of Mary," it is the fear that the Virgin Mary would preach like Christ that incites the princes and priests to rally against her.) The *Digby* play reflects an orthodox position, allowing that women can teach— as did many abbesses and mystical women writers as we can see from records of the age—but not from the pulpit. Here, Mary is clearly represented as a public preacher of scripture in the vernacular language. The play also makes it quite clear that baptism, the Eucharist, and Extreme Unction are sacramental rites that can only be administered by men, priests of the Church. Yet, the play also utilizes the gnostic tradition, expanding on the apostolic role of Mary Magdalene, elaborating and elevating her role, and, therefore, the potential role of women in the Church.

As a saint's play, the issue of conversion is central to the theme, and here, a woman, Mary, is the instrument of conversion, the messenger for the true faith which male authority then sanctions through sacrament. Dream visions, tracing back to the prophetic dreams of the Bible, are also popular in the literature of the Middle Ages, and revelations in dreams were a way of revealing profound spiritual truths. This is why the King of Marseilles' conversion is accomplished through the visit he receives from Mary and two angels during the night. We should note that consistent with Church doctrine, his subsequent baptism is performed by a man, Peter.

Contemporary culture is reflected in the play through the scene of Mary falling into sin in a tavern, seduced by a foppish, sweet-talker, who is the catalyst for her fall into prostitution. While scenes based on Scripture keep orthodox theology in the forefront, scenes of the leaders of Rome worrying about maintaining their positions and controlling possible insurrections add a political dimension; the scenes in the temple of Mohammad not only denounce pagan religion but also add a contemporary flare and comic relief. Ocean voyages are described, humorously using contemporary nautical terms, and the infidels are medieval Muslims, rather than first century A.D. pagans. The medieval Saracens are not only depicted as following Mohammad, but erroneously as idol and devil worshippers, (as are all non-Christians including Jews by the end of the play) to emphasize that they are the enemies of the one truth faith. And of course, we have the historical recognized enemies of Christianity, from Pilate to Tiberius Caesar. The expansive geographic space and multiple eras covered by the play are intended to universalize the message of redemption for the audience.

In the *Digby Mary Magdalene*, deliberate parallels are drawn between Mary Magdalene and the Virgin Mary. The Magdalene is addressed invoking the "Hail Mary" of the Virgin Mother (ll. 1940-44), and while a recluse, she ascends to heaven to be fed by the angels each day, resonating with the Assumption of the Virgin. The comparison of the two women draws both on the obvious oppositions in character, purity versus lasciviousness, sinless versus sinful, as well as on an important congruency recognized between innate virginity and reconstituted virginity. The idea of the reconstituted virgin, or the appropriation of virginal identity, in the late medieval tradition of *mulieres sanctae* frequently evoked the Magdalene. While today, we tend to think of young, chaste women becoming nuns, in the Middle Ages, widows and older women who had raised their children often entered religious houses and took the veil. The ability to reclaim one's virginity to become a bride of Christ was important to these devote women. While Mary Magdalene was barren herself, through her intervention, the queen of Marseilles conceives. We should also not forget the Biblical history of her attending Christ and the apostles. This led to Mary Magdalene being venerated as a maternal, nurturing figure like the Virgin. The adoration of the Virgin and the Magdalene that flourished during the Late Middle Ages, celebrated in pageant and literature, promoted the positive image of the Christian woman that led to greater reverence, respect, and opportunities for women within the Church during that period.

Conclusion

The plays presented here offer a window into the religious beliefs and practices of the laity of the late Middle Ages, illuminating the Catholic teachings circulating in the vernacular language, in the centuries before the Bible was available to be read. The plays put the image of woman in the Catholic Church more than a millennium after the death of Christ in proper perspective, in a time when women's images and roles in the Church were being reconsidered and expanding. Through these late Middle English plays and the history of Marian and Magdalene traditions, we may not only discover more about the Marys' roles in past and contemporary religious practices, we may also better understand how we have arrived at our contemporary views about women's spirituality and women's roles in modern religious institutions.

A note on the modernized translation

The plays were written in stanzaic verses of differing lengths and rhyme schemes. Poetry was not only considered an elevated form of writing, and therefore appropriate for Biblical material, rhymed verse would make it easier for the actors to remember their lines. However, due to changes in pronunciation, the large expansion of English vocabulary and the changing connotation of words, maintaining the lexicon and rhyme scheme of the original text compromises the meaning and clarity of a more contemporary text. In this modernized translation, every attempt has been to preserve the flavor of the language of the period, while creating a text that is available to a modern reader. Line numbers correspond to the texts in the original Middle English.

The *N-Town Mary Play* and Marion materials[1]

Joachim and Anne

Contemplation:[2] Christ protect the congregation
From perils past, present, and future,
And the players performing here, and the pronunciation
Of their words that they might be delivered with gravity and sureness
So that no obstacles obscure the matter,
But profit and please each person present
Who is engaged from beginning to end so that
Christ and all creatures are content with the material.

This material presented is about the Mother of Mercy:
How she was conceived by Joachim and Anne,
And then how she was offered in the temple is briefly covered—
How she then married Joseph, and then, follows the Salutation,
The meeting with Elizabeth and then there is a conclusion,
All covered in a few words, so that it is not tedious
To either lettered or unlearned men.
This is the story; now Jesus preserve you all!

Therefore, peace, I pray all of you that are present here.
Take heed of our oration, of what we shall say.
I commend you to the Lord that is ever omnipotent,
That he governs you in goodness as best he can.
In heaven may we see Him.
Now God that is heaven's king,
Send us all heaven's dear blessing,
And to his tower bring us,
Amen, in love for our fellow man.

---

1   This text includes "Joseph's Doubt," "The Trial of Mary and Joseph," the "Nativity," and "Purification," and "The Assumption of Mary" which are not formally considered part of the *N-Town Mary* play but which are in the *N-Town* collection and found in other play cycles which of the time (*Ludus Coventriae*). Stage directions are in italics. All Latin biblical verse (generally found during scenes of services with an attending priest) are translated into English. [ ] indicates words added or substituted for clarity and more modern syntax or vocabulary. Lines 10-14 list the materials originally considered *The Mary Play*.

2   Contemplation is a type of expositor who introduces the play, its theme, and may comment on the performance.

Ysakar: The priests of God offer sweet incense
Here unto God, and therefore we are holy.
We that minster in God's presence,
No sin should be found in us.
I am Ysakar, prince of priests,
That is charged with ministering on this holiest day,
My charge is to sanctify all the tribes of Israel,
On this the most high and solemn feast day.

We call it the Feast of Incense,
This new feast that we now celebrate for the third year.
Now all Jews must come to Jerusalem
And sacrifice in the temple of God.
The duties of my office demand that I must denounce
Those blessed ones who do not make sacrifice at the temple.
We are the royal priesthood—our wisdom maintained
By fasting, by prayers, by works of charity, and by watchfulness.

Joachim: Now all of us of this country of Galilee
Including the special city of Nazareth,
Must go to Jerusalem to this feast[3]
To make sacrifice to God eternal.
My name is Joachim, a man of means,
"Joachim," means "he that is ready [to serve] God."
So have I been and always shall be,
For I dread the dreadful doom of God.

I am called righteous, you will see why,   50
For I divide my goods among three parties:
One to the temple for those that serve there,
Another for the pilgrims and poor men, the third for those that live with me.
Every priest in this wide world should do the same,
Give a portion of his goods, certainly;
A part to his parishioners that have slid into poverty,
A third part kept for him and his household.

But blessed wife Anne, I truly dread
Making sacrifice in the temple this time,

---

3   Despite the fact that these plays were written in Catholic England in the fifteenth century where
    Jews have been exiled for centuries, the plays demonstrate a knowledge of Jewish custom and ritual,
    presumably primarily from the use of the source materials passed down through oral and written
    tradition. The overlay of Catholic conventions from reference to the Trinity to the Five Joys of
    Mary while observing Judaic rituals, as well as Christian interpretation of these rituals, enhances
    the transition from Judaic to Christian rule, and a reading of the New Testament as fulfillment
    of the Old. Given that the Jews were expelled from England in 1290 by royal edict, the lack of
    anti-Semitism in the early Mary plays is worth remarking. Anti-Semitism is clearly reflected in "The
    Assumption of Mary" and the *Digby Magdalene*.

Because we have borne no fruit.*   * are childless
I greatly fear the priests will despise me,
And we will be greatly slandered among the tribes,
But I promise to endure this with as much meekness as I can.
If in his mercy He would send us a child,
We would offer it up in the temple to be God's man.

Anne: Your heartfelt words make tears trickle down my face.
Certainly, sweet husband, the fault is in me.
My name is Anne, that is to say, "grace."
We do not know how gracious God's will shall be revealed to us.
We have prophecies that a woman shall bear Christ.
If God send us fruit, and it be a maid child,
I vow with all reverence to his majesty,
That she shall be her lady in waiting and graciously serve her.

Joachim: Let it be as God wills it; there is nothing more.
I will take two turtledoves with me to sacrifice,
And I beseech you, wife, whenever we meet again
That we let his great mercy make us happy.

Anne: I tremble with dread and sorrow at your words!
Thrice I kiss you as I sigh in sadness,
And I entrust you to the mercy of God,
And though we depart in sorrow, may God make that meeting joyful.

Senior of the tribe: Worshipful sir Joachim, are you ready now?
All your kindred have come to support you,
They will do sacrifice in the temple with you,
For men hold you in great esteem.

Joachim: God may comfort all the sinful, sick, and sorrowful.
I wish I were as men report of me.
In God's name let us all make our way forth.
Ah, Anne, Anne, Anne, God shield us from shame!

Anne: Now I am left alone; I weep in sorrow.
Ah, husband, may God bring you safely [home to me]
And keep you from shame and sorrow.
I cannot cease weeping until I see you again.

Senior: Prince of our priests, if it be pleasing to you,
We meekly come to make our sacrifice.
Ysakar: God's blessing to you young and old!
Devoutly we will begin the service.

*They shall sing this sequence "Blessed be the Blessed Trinity," and at this time,
Ysakar and his priest incense the altar, and they make their offering.*

Ysakar: Now come forth, sirs, and all make your offering,
You that are worthy to make sacrifice.
Wait awhile, sir! What are you doing here?   100
You and your wife are barren and bare!
Neither of you is fruitful and never were.
How dare you presume to appear and blasphemy the fruitful?
It is a sign that you are cursed!
Therefore, I refuse your offering with great indignation!

He refuses Joachim's sacrifice.

The barren are not allowed among these people.
Come forward and make offering all of you here.
You, Joachim, I charge thee to depart from the temple!⁴

Ysakar returns to the congregation weeping.

Then with God's holy words I shall bless you.

The priest sings, "Our help in the name of the Lord."

Chorus: Who made heaven and earth.

Priest: Blessed be the name of the Lord.

Chorus: From this time on and forevermore.

Ysakar: The divine one, God, bless you,
Father, and Son, and Holy Spirit.⁵

Chorus: Amen.

Blesses all with the sign of the cross, and the people leave the temple.

Ysakar: Now you are blessed by God and man.
Return homeward again all of you.

---

4   Ysakar should not be seen as an evil or malicious character; he does as the law commands him to do in
     banishing Joachim; medieval Catholics would see this as excommunication. Joachim will accept this
     sentence and the shame it carries. He chooses to exile himself from his wife and community because
     of it, and while exiled prays for God's forgiveness for whatever offenses he has committed. He never
     blames God nor considers his treatment unjust.

5   The Trinity references, ll. 115 and 120, are the first blending of Christian and Judaic law by a Jewish
     figure of authority in the play. In line 70, Anne has spoken of the coming of Christ being prefigured,
     linking the Old and New Testament.

And we, the priests, shall stay
To serve God in his Trinity.

Joachim: Ah, merciful Lord, what is this life?
What have I done, Lord, to receive this castigation?
By heaven, I dare not go home to my wife,
Among my neighbors, I may not live for shame!
Ah, Anne, Anne, Anne, all our joy is turned to grief!
I am now exiled from your blessed fellowship,
Once you hear of this foul fame,
Sorrow will slay you, seeing me so defamed!

But since God sends us these trials, we must suffer them.
So now I will go and abide with my shepherds,
And live forevermore with them in sorrow and dread.
Shame makes many a man hide his head.
How are you, my fellows? Little pride can be found in you.[6]
I truly want to know how you and my beasts are doing.

Shepherd 1: Welcome here blessed master! We pasture them well.
They are full of life and greatly multiply.
How are you doing master? You look heavy of heart.
How does our mistress? Does she sit at home and sew?

Joachim: To hear you speak of her truly breaks my heart,
How she and I do, God himself knows.
God lifts up the meek; He overthrows the proud.
Go, do as you like! See that your beasts do not stray.

Shepherd 2: Master, after great sorrow, may great grace grow.
Though we are simple men, we will pray for you as best we can.

Shepherd 3: Yes, the sorrowful are in need of our prayers.
Kneeling, we will pray for you,
That God in his goodness will send you aid quickly,
And soon redress your sorrow.

Joachim: I am not worthy, Lord, to look up to heaven.
My sinful steps have poisoned the ground.   150
I, the most loathsome being living, You the highest Lord in his seven seats.
What are You, Lord? What am I but more wretched than a dog.
You have sent me shame that wounds my heart!
I thank You for all the prosperity I have had before now.

---

6   Joachim is Job-like in trying to deal with his tribulations. He seeks refuge among his shepherds,
     considered the humblest of people; hence, they are described without pride.

That is a token that You love me, so that now I am bound to You.
You say that You are with them that are suffering tribulations.

Therefore, whoever has them, he need not to have worry;
My sorrow gives me fear that I have done You some offense.
Punish me Lord, and spare my wife Anne,
That sits and is filled with great sorrow in my absence.
None can profit* but by prayers to your person.   *succeed
Prostrate in prayer, I weep before You.
Keep in mind our devotion to your great magnificence.
And my loving wife, Anne, Lord, keep her in thy mercy.

Anne: Ah, mercy, Lord! Mercy, mercy, mercy!
We are the most sinful! That is shown us by the sorrow You send.
Why do You do this to my husband, Lord? Why, why, why?
As for my bareness, if You wanted to You could amend it tomorrow.
If it pleased You in your mercy, I bear witness.
I shall keep my vow while I live and endure.
I fear that I have offended You, my heart is full of sorrow.
Most meekly I pray for your pity, that You will end this suffering.

The angel descends, the heavens sing, "Let the heavens praise, ringing in the joy, let the angles sing in solemn glory."

Joachim: In God's name, what are you that makes me so afraid?
There is a light about me, as if the world were on fire!

Angel: I am an angel of God that has come to make you glad.
God is pleased with the alms you offer and has heard your prayer.
He sees your shame, your reproof, and your bright tears.
God is the avenger of sin and does not hate human nature.
Whose womb he has passed over and made barren,
He does so to show both his might and mercy.

You saw that Sara was barren ninety years:[7]
She had a son Isaac to whom God gave his blessing.
Rachel also endured the same pain.
She had a son Joseph that became king of Egypt.
Never was there written [a story of] a stronger man except Sampson,
Or a holier except Samuel, so it is said.
Yet their mothers were both barren in the beginning—
The conception by them was considered miraculous.

---

7   Lines 181 to 191 resolve the Old Testament as prefiguring the New within this play. The biblical cycle
     now moves from Old Testament to New Testament materials, using this play to unify the Testaments.

And in the same way, Anne, thy blessed wife,
She shall bear a child that shall be called Mary,
Who will be blessed in her body and have five joys,[8]
And [be] specially graced by the Holy Ghost.
She shall be solemnly offered at the temple,
No sin shall befall her,*   *she shall be a chaste virgin
And just as she shall be borne of a barren body,
So shall she bear Jesus without knowing man,
He shall be the Savior of all mankind.
When you come to the Golden Gate in Jerusalem,
Have this sign in mind. You shall meet Anne thy wife,
I shall tell her the same to relieve her sorrow.   200

Joachim: I shall never forget the incomparable comfort brought me today,
My sorrow could not have been greater, but now my joy is even more!
I shall make my way home in haste, before it gets even later.
Ah, Anne, blessed be the child that shall be born of you!
Farewell now my shepherds, govern yourselves wisely.

Shepherd 1: Have you heard good tidings, master? Then we are glad.

Joachim: Praise God for me, for I am not worthy.

Shepherd 2: In faith, sir, we shall with all our humble souls.

Shepherd 3: It would be good for one of us to go with you.

Joachim: No, abide here with your beasts in God's blessing.

Shepherd 1: We shall make merry now that this is settled,
You shall hear us sing for a mile as you make your way.

Anne: Alas, for my husband's absence, I am full of woe!
Whatever may happen, I will seek him.
I do not know which way he has gone on this earth.
Father in Heaven, for mercy, I fall at your feet.

Angel: Anne, I was just with your husband.
I, the angel of God, bore him glad tidings,
And as I said to him, so I say to you;
God has heard thy prayer and thy weeping.
And you should meet him humbly at the Golden Gate,
And in great joy return to your house.
In due course, you shall conceive and bear a child.

---

8   The five joys of Mary are the Annunciation, the Nativity, the Resurrection, the Ascension, and the
Assumption.

Who shall be called Mary, and Mary shall bear Jesus.
Who shall be Savior of the world and all of us.
After great sorrow is even greater joy.
Now, thus have I said to you in my message,
Go in our Lord's name and in God rejoice.

Anne: Now, [I am] blessed by our Lord and all his works forevermore.
All heaven and earth may bless you for this!
I am so full of joy that I do not now what to say!
No tongue can tell the joy that is in me:
I am to bear a child that shall [bring] all man's bliss,
And have my husband again—who could have more joy?
Certainly, no creature on earth is granted more mercy.
I shall hurry to the gate so that I arrive before him.

   The angel returns to heaven.

Ah, blessed be our Lord! I see my husband.
I shall creep toward him on my knees.

Joachim: Ah, gracious wife, Anne, now you shall be fruitful!
The joy of this meeting makes me weep in my soul!
Have this pure kiss and keep it with you.
In God's name now let us go home to our house, wife.

Anne: There was never a joy that had affected me so deeply!
Husband, now we see that God has truly graced us,
Truly.

Joachim: Yes, and if we lived well [before now according to Thee],
I pray your mercy Lord,
So will we live forevermore
And by thy grace be even more holy.

Anne: Husband, I urge that we now go home.   250
Straight home to our place
To thank God that sits on his throne
That has sent us his grace.

The Presentation of Mary
in the Temple

Contemplation: Ladies and gentlemen, you have had shown to you previously,
Of Joachim and Anne, of their holy meeting together,
Of how our Lady was conceived and how she was born.
For lack of time we passed over that briefly,
And now proceed to how our Lady,
At a tender young age, was offered at the temple.
Now we shall begin with this solemn matter,
Let the Mother of Mercy help us.

As a three-year-old child, here she shall appear
To all the people that are present.
And you shall hear of her great grace—
How with grace she always lived
In accordance with God's will.
We will show this holy matter,
How she fared until she was fourteen years old.
Now I ask all of you that are in this place
To refrain from speaking.

> *Joachim and Anne with our Lady—a child of three years, dressed all in white—*
> *between them, present her to the temple.*

Joachim: Blessed be our Lord! We have fair fruit now.
Anne, wife, you will remember
That we made a holy vow to God
That our first child should be a servant of God.
Our daughter Mary is now three years old.
Therefore, to the three person in one God, let us present her.
The younger she is when she is brought to the temple, the better it seems to me.
And if we wait too long in honoring our vow to God, we might be chastised.

Anne: It shall be as you say, husband.
Let us take Mary, our daughter, between us
And proceed with her to the temple.
Daughter, the angel told us that you should be a queen!
Will you go see the Lord that shall be your husband
And learn to love Him and live your life according to Him?
Tell your father and me here your answer, let's see—
Will you be a pure maiden and God's wife?[9]

---

9   Mary is being asked if she will be a pure virgin of the temple of God. Remembering that she is Jewish,
     for the Catholic audience, the allusion is to choosing to become a nun or bride of Christ.

Mary: Father and mother, if it pleases you,
As you have made your vow so truly will I
To be God's chaste servant while life is in me.
But I will never be worthy to be God's wife!
I am the simplest creature ever born.
I have heard you say: "God should have a sweet mother."
That I believe. Grant me the mercy to see her
And allow me to lay my hands under her fair feet!

Mary kneels to God.

Joachim: Certainly, daughter, this is well said.
You answer as if you were twenty years old.

Anne: I am well pleased with your speech, Mary.
Can you go alone? Let's see. Be bold!

Mary: You will now behold me [as I] go into God's house.
I am as joyful as I can be to go henceforth.

Joachim: Wife, I am filled with great joy as I behold our daughter.

Anne: So am I, wise husband. Now, in God's name, we will go.

Joachim: Sir prince of priests, if it pleases you,   50
We that were barren, God has sent to us a child.
We vowed to offer her into God's service;
Here is the same maid, Mary most mild.

Ysakar: Joachim, I remember how I excommunicated you.
I am very glad that God has given you this grace
To be among the fruitful. Now be restored [to this holy community].
Come, sweet Mary, come! You have a gracious face!

Joachim, kneeling to God, saying:

Joachim: Now Father and Son and Holy Ghost,
In the Three Persons of God,
We offer to Thee, Lord most mighty,
Our daughter to be thy servant forevermore.

Anne: Henceforth are we forever bound to you.
Mary, in this holy place, we shall leave you,
In God's name, now we shall go.
Our Father, our priest, does call you.

Mary: Certainly, mother, if it pleases you, first I will take my leave
Of my father and you, my mother.
I have a Father in heaven; this I believe.
Now, good father, with that Father bless me.

Joachim: In the name of the Father, the Son, and the Holy Spirit.

Mary: Amen. Now you, good mother.

Anne: In the name of the Father, the Son, and the Holy Spirit.

Mary: Amen.
Now our Lord, bless you both,
My father and mother, for this.
I beseech you that I may humbly kiss you.
Forgive me if ever I made you angry.

She embraces them and kisses her father and mother.

Joachim: No, daughter, you never offended God nor man.
Beloved is that Lord who keeps you.

Anne: Sweet daughter, think upon your mother, Anne,
Your grieving cuts deep into my heart.

Mary: Father and mother, I shall pray for you and cry[10]
To God sincerely with all my heart.
Bless me day and night wherever you lie down your heads and sleep.
Good father and mother be joyful.

Joachim: Ah, who has ever had such a child?
Has there ever yet been such a creature born?
She is so gracious; she is so mild:
So children should always be to their mothers and fathers.

Anne: Then they should be blessed and greatly please God.
Husband, if it please you, let us not leave
Until Mary is received into the temple above.
I would not see her fail for the world.

---

10   In the Middle Ages, the tears of women, were seen as having special power to intercede with God for
     the sinner, recalling the tears of the Marys at the crucifixion of Christ.

Ysakar: Come, good Mary. Come babe, I call thee:
Direct your steps carefully into this place.
You shall be a daughter of the eternal God.
If you can ascend the fifteen steps,
It is a miracle if you can do so. God defend you!
From Babylon to heavenly Jerusalem, this is the way:
Every man that thinks to amend his life   100
Remember the fifteen psalms this maid recites.

Mary recites the Gradual Psalms (119–33), which are the fifteen steps between the Beautiful Gate and the Gate of Nicanor in Herod's Temple.

Mary: The first spiritually demands,
That I wholly desire to be with God.
I cry to God when I am in trouble,
And the Lord quickly hears me.[11]

The second is study, very humbly inquiring
How I shall know God's will.
I have lifted my eyes to the mountains of heaven,
From whence He will come help me.

The third is joy contemplating
That we shall all be saved.
I am glad of these tidings said to me.
Now shall we go into God's house.

The fourth is the humble obedience that is due,
To Him that is above the seven planets:
I have set my eyes on You
That dwells above the skies in heaven.

The fifth is proper confession,
So that we will not be without God,
So that God always dwells within us,
Lest by misadventure our enemies should swallow us up.

The sixth is confidence in God's strength alone,
For all grace streams forth from Him:
They that trust in God, as at Mount Sion,
Shall not be driven out but shall always dwell in Jerusalem.

The seventh is unwavering faith in the eternal,
In our Lord's grace and mercy.

---

11   The Latin follows each verse in the play.

When out Lord delivered us from our captivity [in Sion],
Then we are made joyful.

The eighth is contempt of the pride within us,
For Him that that has created all mankind.
Unless our Lord dwells within their house,
They who have built it labor in vain.

The ninth is childish fear, indeed,
With a never-ending, longing love for our Lord.
Blessed are all that fear God,
Who follow his holy ways.

The tenth is mighty endurance of carnal temptation,
For the fleshy sights are fierce and deadly.
Often youth has struggled with such vexation,
As God has seen, now says Israel.

The eleventh is the accusatory confession of iniquity,
Which is extremely painful.
I have cried to thee from the depths, Lord!
Lord, quickly hear my humble voice!

The twelfth is sweet and meek humility,
In man's soul within and without;
Lord, my heart is not raised on high*   *filled with pride
Nor do my eyes look about.

The thirteenth is faith always,   150
With holy deeds done openly;
Lord, Remember David
And all his gentleness.

The fourteen is brotherly love, certainly,
That nourishes love in all creatures:
How good and joyful it is
To dwell as one in brotherhood.

The fifteenth is grace, bringing all together as one,
Which seems to me to be a sign of God's love.
See now that we bless our Lord,
We all that are God's servants.

Ysakar: Gracious Lord this is a marvelous thing
That we all see here in our presence!

A babe of three years, so young,
Who comes up these steps so righteously!
It is a high miracle, and by God's might,
No doubt she shall be filled with grace.

Mary: Holy father, presently I beseech you,
Say how I shall be instructed in God's house.

Ysakar: Daughter, God has given us ten commandments,
Which, briefly to say, can be comprehended in two parts.
They must be kept by all Christian men
Or else they shall dwell in eternal pain.*   *the damnation of Hell
You must love your sovereign God above all men.
He loved you first; love Him in return,
For in love, in his likeness, He made you.

Love Father, Son, and Holy Ghost:
Love God the Father, for He gives strength.
Love God the Son, for He gives the wisdom you need.
Love God the Holy Ghost, for He gives love and light.
Three persons in one God, that love is right.
With all thy heart, with all thy soul, with all thy mind,
And with all the strength that dwells within you,
Love your fellow Christians always, as you would love yourself.

You should hate nothing but the devil and sin:
God bids you to love your earthly enemies.
And as for [all you who are] here, this is how you shall proceed:
You must serve and worship God here daily,
With prayer, with grace and mercy.
See you keep yourself well nourished
So that you can labor steadfastly,
[That is the way to] spiritual and physical reward.
Five maidens will dwell with you,
To offer consolation whenever you are in need.

Mary: This way of life is pleasing to me,
I beseech you to inform me of their names.

Ysakar: The first is Meditation,
Contrition, Compassion, Chastity,
And the holy maid Fruition.[12]   200
You shall perform your work with the companionship of these blessed maidens.

---

12 These are internal qualities of Mary allegorically externalized as companions. They are first mentioned
  as her attendants in the apocryphal *Pseudo-Matthew*.

Mary: I feel I am not worthy
To be in this holy fellowship.
Sweet sisters, I kneel to all of you.
I beseech you for your charity in receiving me.

Ysakar: They shall, and in addition, daughter,
Indeed, there shall be seven priests,
To hear your confession and to teach and minister to you,
To teach you God's laws and to read Scripture to you.

Mary: Father, I would gladly learn their names.
Ysakar: They are Discretion, Devotion, Dedication, and Deliberation,
They shall diligently attend you
With Declaration, Determination, and Divination.
Now, you maidens proceed to do your duty
And look that you tend this child tenderly.
And you, sirs, kneel, and I shall give you God's blessing,
In the name of the Father, Son, and Holy Spirit.

She leaves with the priests, and all the virgins say "Amen."

Mary: I ask you, father and mother, that you commend me.
Blessed be the time that you brought me hither.

Joachim: Daughter, you must defend the Father of our faith,
Who through his might made all things from nothing.

Anne: Mary, may He send solas* into your soul,   *bliss/joy
Through whose wisdom all this world was made.
Let us now go hence gracious husband,
For we have now been brought out of woe.

Joachim and Anne return home.

Mary: May you be brought home by the Holy Ghost.

To the virgins:

Sisters, you can go do what you will:
All my thought is to first serve God.
I fall on my knees before this holy altar.

Lord, seven petitions I beseech of You here:
The first, that I may keep thy love and thy law;
The second, to love my fellow Christians as dearly as myself;
The third, to keep myself from all that You hate;

The fourth, to know all the virtues that please You;
The fifth, to obey every law of the temple;
The sixth, that all people serve Thee with reverence,
That no fault can be found in this holy temple.

The seventh, Lord, I ask you with great fear,
That I may see once in my life
That lady that shall bear God's Son,
That I may serve her with my five wits,*   *senses
If it pleases you otherwise I would not desire it.
Prostrate, I weep and offer prayers for these favors.
O, my God, devotion dwells deep within me,
Driving my heart to wake in Thee even though my body sleeps.

*The angels bring manna like confections in a cup of gold. The heavens sing, and
the angel says:*

Angel: Meekest of maids do not marvel at my ministrations!
I am a good angel sent from God Almighty
With angel's food for your sustenance,
Receive it, it will sustain your physical body.
We angels will serve you day and night,   250
Feeding you here, in God's name.
We shall teach you the library of God's luminous laws
To instruct you in your humility.

Mary: I have no means to thank the Lord sufficiently.
I shall feed myself with the food my Lord has sent.
I find all kinds of sweet fragrances in this food!
I never tasted any so sweet or fragrant.

Angel: Thereby, each day you shall be content*   *satiated/fed
Angels shall appear to you at all hours.

Mary: Mercy, my maker, what does this mean?
I am the simplest creature living.

Angel: In your name Mary, we have five letters:
M – Maid, most merciful and humble of mind.
A – Averter undoing the anguish that Adam began.
R – Regina, Queen reigning endlessly over all realms on earth and in heaven.
I – Innocent by the inheritance of Jesse', the chosen, people;
A – Advocate most pure, your ancestor Anne.
Heaven and hell here bend down on their knees
When your holy name is said, Mary!

Mary: I tremble in fear hearing this commendation!
Good sweet angel, why would you say this?

Angel: You shall have hereafter a salutation
That will surpass this. It is said among us [that]
The Deity shall determine and discuss that deed.*   *the Incarnation
You shall never be left alone, Lady

Mary: I cry thee mercy, Lord, and kiss the earth,
Recommending myself to that Godhead, triune on throne.

> *She kisses the ground. Angels come and go with various presents. And in time, they*
> *shall sing in heaven this hymn, "Jesus, crown of virgins." After, a priest comes from*
> *the bishop, Ysakar, with a present and the priest says:*

Priest: Prince of our priests, Ysakar by name,
Has sent [food to] you from his own table
And bade that you should now eat
Without shame and no longer fast.

Mary: Recommend me to my father, sir, and may God reward him.
I shall soon send these dishes back to him.
I shall take them to my sisters; I believe they have more need than I;
God's bounty is always closer to his servants than we think.

Sisters, our holy father Ysakar
Hath just now sent us food from his pantry.
Eat heartily of it! I pray you do not hold back,
And if anything be left, I ask you,
That the leftovers be given to the poor.
Gladly, if I may, I would do merciful deeds:
How poor folk survive, God knows—
I will forever have pity on them.

Contemplation: Good people, here you have seen
Our Lady's presentation in the temple,
She was never occupied with vain, earthly pursuits,
But always busy in holy occupations.

And we beseech you for your forgiveness
That we passed over these matters quickly.
If they were done with sufficient care,   300
Each one would fill a whole day.

Now we will proceed to her betrothal.
Which occurred at the time she was fourteen years of age.
We cannot take a sufficient enough pause for that time to elapse,
So have patience with us, we beseech you.

And soon thereafter,
The Parliament of Heaven you shall see,
And how God's Son shall become man
And of the Salutation* after   *Annunciation
By God's holy grace.

The Marriage of Mary and Joseph

Ysakar, the bishop, enters.

Ysakar: Listen lords, both high and low born,
And tenderly take heed of my speech,
Be both humble and meek, and present yourself before your bishop.
For I am the lord that made this law.
So now listen with obedient hearts,
Bring forth, as you should, your maidens to wed
That are past fourteen years of age.
The law of God commands this:
That at fourteen years of age,
Every damsel, whosoever she is,
To increase the fruit of our nation [by bearing children],
Shall be brought here, as is custom,
To be married.

Joachim: Anne, my gentle spouse, hear now
How that the bishop has delivered his decree,
That what[ever] man who has a daughter in his house
That is past fourteen years of age,
Must bring her into the temple
To wed a spouse, so I heard him proclaim.
Therefore, our right good and sweet daughter,
Must be led to the temple
Right away.

Anne: Sir, I grant that it must be so.
We cannot act against the law.
Let us go together with her.
That is the best thing to do.

Joachim: Sir bishop, as you have commanded,
We have brought our dear daughter here:
Mary, my sweet daughter, she has reached the age.
She is fourteen years old.

Ysakar: Welcome, Joachim into my dwelling,
As well as both Anne, thy wife, and Mary pure.
Now, Mary child, listen to the law,
And choose a spouse to be thy partner,
So that you may fulfill the law.

Mary: I will never oppose the law,
But I will never engage a man's fellowship;
I will live always in chastity,
By the grace of God's will.

Ysakar: Ah, fair maid, why do you say that?
What do you mean that you will live chastely?
Why will you not wed?
Tell me the reason, and quickly at that!

Mary: Certainly, my father and mother,
Truly before I was born,
They were both barren, and she was past the age of fertility.
In the end, they came to the temple
To offer sacrifice.
Because they had neither fruit or child,
They were reproached for being wicked and wild.   50
All men despised them,
They were reviled and shamed.

My father and my mother, they wept grievously,
Their hearts were heavy because of this affair!
Tearfully they prayed,
That God would help them and send them a seed.
They promised that the child should lead her life
Serving in God's temple forevermore
And worship God in love and dread.
Then God, full of grace,
He heard their prayer of longing,
And sent them both seed and flower.
When I was born in their bower,
I was offered to the temple.
There I promised, as my heart willed me,
To serve my God with boundless love.
Purity and chastity enwrap my heart,
Earthly creature can never drive them out.
You should not in any way
Reprove a pure life.
As I tell you, this is the reason
That I will never have intercourse with a man.
I will dwell in the service of God forever.
I will never have any other mate.

Ysakar: Ah, mercy God! These wise words
Of this fair, chaste maid,
They trouble my heart in many ways.

Her wit is great, desiring
To live chastely in God's service.
No man can blame or censor her.
Yet the law still requires
That all should be wedded.
It is clearly put forth:
The law says and bids
That after a life of purity all maids
Must prepare themselves for marriage.
God deliver us from doubt!

This answer greatly troubles me,
To make a vow to the people is allowed under law.
We pray and tithe according to Scripture,
And it is necessary that we observe our law.
To render a decision is daunting to me.
Therefore, I call the council to consider this case.
The old and wise will be especially helpful:
I beseech you to say as you advise in this.

Priest: It would be hard indeed to break our law and custom![13]   100
And on the other hand, to go against Scripture,
You must indeed take care in passing such a grave judgment.

Doubtless, this matter is complicated and obscure.*   *enigmatic, difficult
Here, I assure you, this is my advice,
That we all pray to God for instruction,
For through prayer, great knowledge can be obtained,
And this is the advice with which I counsel you.

Ysakar: Truly, your counsel is good, just, and wholesome.
And, as you have said, so shall it be.
I charge you, brothers and sisters: come here
And together to God we will now pray,
That it may please his infinite deity,
And that He send us wisdom in this.
Let each man meekly fall down on his knee,
And we shall sing "Come Creator Spirit."

They sing "Come Creator Spirit" and when they are done—

---

13 This movement from Judaic law into Christianity and the accompanying value in the virginity of
    Christ and Mary is often spoken of by St. Paul, as in 1 Cor 7. As the Holy Orders of priests is
    established and finds precedence through the apostles, such a presentation of Mary establishes a
    precedent for women taking the habit.

Ysakar: Now, Lord God of Lords, wisest of all,
I pray to you, Lord, kneeling on knee.
I cry and call with a heavy heart.
Direct me in how to deal with this grave uncertainty.

Angel: Thy prayer is heard in the high heavenly hall.
God has sent me down here to you
To tell you what you should do.
And how thou should be ruled in each instance.
Take care and heed [what I say].
This is God's own bidding:
That all the kinsmen of David the king
Bring their due offering to the temple
Bearing white branches in their hands.
Pay close attention to what they offer at this time!
All shall bring branches in their hands for you to take.
Look whose branch does blossom and bloom,
For he shall be the maiden's mate.

Ysakar: I thank you, Lord, humbly
I shall carry out your word without question.
I shall send for them, far and near,
Undertaking to carry out your will.
It shall be done!
Hark messenger, I command you,
Go on your way to David's kinsman.
Tell them to come and make offering this same day
And to bring white branches with them.

Messenger: Listen to me, men of all station,
That are kindred* of king David!   *of the lineage
My lord, the bishop, has sent for you
To come to the temple with your offering.
He commands that you hurry, for he is prepared
To receive you when you come.
Furthermore, he commands that every one of you
Bring a fair white branch held high
In your hands.   150
I pray you, do not tarry!
I say to you, my lord
Is fully prepared
To receive you.

Joseph: I have labored greatly in my life.
My occupation has taken me to many places;

Because of the infirmities of age, I cannot hurry on that journey.
I thank You for your grace, great God.

David's Kin 1: What grieves you so, Joseph?
That you lie here on the ground?

Joseph: Age and feebleness do so embrace me
That I can neither stand or go forth.

David's Kin 2: We are commanded by the bishop's messenger
That every man of David's kin*   *Jewish man
Must go to offer a wand[14] at the temple;
Therefore, let us go forth.

Joseph: There is no need for me to travel.
My friends, I pray you, go on your way.

David's Kin 3: Yes, come with us, Joseph, I urge you,
And learn what the bishop will say.

David's Kin 4: There is a maid who is named Mary.
It is said she is the daughter of Joachim.
They will test to determine which worthy and doughty man
Will have her to marry.

Joseph: Bless me, I do not understand
What the priest of priests means
By having every man capable of being married
Bring a wand with him, that is not meant for me.
I have been a virgin all my life and ever will be[15]
And now to be married, a man would think
It a strange thing for an old man to take a young wife.

But nevertheless, no doubt, we must go forth to town.
Now neighbors and kinsmen, let's go forth.
I shall take a wand in my hand and cast off my gown,
If I fall, then I shall groan in pain.
Whosoever takes away my staff, I say he is my foe.
You, men that run fast, hurry before me!

---

14 The branch, rod, or wand—the terms are used interchangeably—is meant to have phallic associations and suggest the fertility demanded of the union of man and wife. Here the lily white branch (l. 243) connotes virginity counter to the fertility tradition and prefigures the virginal conception through God and the Holy Spirit who descends to sit upon the branch.

15 In some sources and analogues, Joseph is a widow with grown sons. See for example, *The Infancy Gospel of James* and the *Ludus Coventrie* plays.

I am old and also cold. Walking pains me.
Moreover, as I hold my staff here, I wish this journey were done.

Ysakar: Sirs, you shall understand
The reason we are gathered here
And why each of you was asked to bring a wand.
God has directed us [to do so].
Here is a young maid to be married.
You shall all bring your rods to me,
And on whoever's rod the Holy Spirit sits,
He shall be the husband of this maid.

    They bring the branches.

Joseph: It shall not me, I bet!
I shall stay hid behind.   200
God knows that I wish I were home in my cottage.
Truly, I am ashamed to be seen.

David's Kin 1: I come here to worship my Lord God;
Here to proffer the offering as is my due.
I have brought a fair white branch in my hand,
My lord, sir bishop, at your bidding.

David's Kin 2: Indeed, I, who am of David's kin, have come.
I bring a fair white branch in hand.
My lord, the bishop, by your own behest,
Here I offer this branch,
As you have commanded.

David's Kin 3: I, also, have readily brought
A fair and white branch in my hand,
Graciously, as requested.

David's Kin 4: I am the fourth of David's kin,
And I honor God with my offering.
This fair white branch is my offering.
I trust to God for my succor.
Come with thy offering Joseph
And bring forth yours as we have ours;
You stray behind too long, certainly.
Why do you not come forth into God's dwelling place?
For shame, come on man.

Joseph: Yes, yes, come! With God's help, I will come!
But I am so old and infirm

That both my legs are about to fold [under me]—
I am nearly lame!

Ysakar: Mercy Lord! I cannot see a sign!
It is best that we enter into prayer again.

[Heavenly] Voice: Truly, he to whom the maid should be married
Has not yet presented his rod.

Ysakar: What, Joseph? Why do you lag behind?
Certainly sir, that is shameful!

Joseph: Sir, I can't find my rod!
Truthfully, it seems shameful to me to come here.

Ysakar: Come hence!

Joseph: Sir, it is difficult for the lame to hurry forth.
Truly, I come as fast as I can!

Ysakar: Sir, offer up your rod, in God's name!
Why do you not do as men ask of you?

Joseph: Now, worshipping God in Heaven,
I offer this lily[16] white branch,
Praying the Lord of gracious speech,
With heart, with wit, with mind, and strength.
And as he made the seven planets,
This simple, small offering I make,
That He may receive for his worship.
This branch is ready to do his worship.
Lord God I pray You,   250
Take good heed of what is in my heart
And not my sinful deed.
Reward me for the duties I have performed,
As it pleases You.
I may not lift my hands up high.
Lo, what do you see now?

Priest: Mercy, mercy Lord we cry!
We see you are blessed by God!

All cry, "mercy, mercy!"

———————

16   Symbolizes his virginity.

Gracious God on heaven's throne,
Your works are wondrous!
Here we may see a marvelous one—
Dead stock bears fine flowers.
Don't be dismayed Joseph.
You should be filled with happiness and joy.
I see by this miracle,
You must wed a maid.
Her name is Mary.

Joseph: What, should I wed? God forbid!
I am an old man, God help me.
To live with a wife now I dread.
It would not be sport or game.

Ysakar: You cannot act against God, Joseph!
God wills that you have a wife.
This fair maid shall be thy wife;
She is humble and white as bread.

Joseph: Should I have her? You should destroy my life!
Alas, dear God, should I now become a passionate man?
An old man may never thrive
With a young wife, God save me![17]
No, no sir, let is be!
Should I now, being doughty in my old age?
If I should have her, she will beat me,
Hoodwink me and chide me about trifles,
As it is often said.[18]

Ysakar: Joseph, now I say to you,
God has assigned her to you.
What God will have you do, would you say no to?
Our Lord God wills that it be so.

Joseph: I may not go against my God;
I will be her warden and keeper forever.
But fair maiden, I pray thee,
Keep yourself chaste, as I will me.
I am an old man.
Therefore, sir bishop, I will have you know,

---

17 May-December marriages, old men with young women, were a common contrivance for stories of cuckoldry/adultery in the Middle Ages.
18 Misogynistic ideas of how husbands will suffer under their wives offered by many (male) authorities and writers.

We shall never lie together in bed,
For certainly, sweet maiden,
An old man may not be a passionate lover.

Bishop: This holiest virgin you shall now marry.
Your rod flourishes fairest, as men may see.
The Holy Ghost sits on that bough   300
Now let us all praise the Trinity.

They sing "Blessed be the Trinity"

Joseph, will you have this maiden for your wife,
And honor and keep her as you ought to do?

Joseph: Nay, sir, I may not prosper,
Nor do I have need of this.

Ysakar: Joseph, it is God's will that is should be!
Say after me, as required by our law.

Joseph: Sir, I will bend and perform his will
For everything ought to be according to his will.

Bishop Ysakar and then Joseph.

Ysakar: Say then after me: "Here I take thee, Mary, to be my wife,
To have, to hold, as God by his will commands us,
Between us for the rest of our lives
To love you as myself, I plight my troth."

Then to Mary the bishop says,

Mary, will you have this man,
And keep yourself for him for the rest of your life?

Mary: In the most tender way I can, father,
With my five wits.*   *five senses

Ysakar: Joseph, with this ring, now wed thy wife,
And take her hand.

Joseph: Sir with this ring, I promptly wed her
And take her now for my mate.

Ysakar: Mary, maid, without more argument,
You must take him as your spouse.

Mary: I will lead my life in chastity.
And never forsake him,
But will live with him forever.
And gentle spouse, as you have said,
Let me live as a virgin.
I shall be true, forever and always,
Be not dismayed.

Ysakar: Here is the holiest marriage that ever was in the world![19]
We will now sing the high names of our Lord.
We will record this solemn deed devoutly,
"Gracious chorus of the Lord proclaim now the names of the Most High."

Now all shall go home in God's name.
Maidens, since you dwelt together until now,
It would greatly sadden your hearts
And be a shame to let her go forth alone.
You shall bless the time that she was born,
Now accompany her to her home.

Mary: I fall before you seeking your blessing, father.

Ysakar: He that has no ending blesses you:
In the name of the Father, Son and Holy Spirit.

Joseph, you are of old age,
And thy wife is young,
And as we read in the old sages,
Many men speak slander [concerning such arrangements];
Therefore to assuage rumors,
So that your good reputation may endure,
Three damsels shall dwell with you in your home   350
And always be in your wife's company.
I shall call on these three here.
Susanne shall be the first;
Rebecca shall be the second, Sephore the third
That shall go with thee. Make sure the three of you
Never forsake this maiden.

Susanne: Sir, at your will, I am ready
To go with this maiden.

Rebecca: I will fulfill your bidding
And follow this fair and worthy maiden.

19   Ysakar blessing this chaste union marks a deviation from Judaic law. The ceremony itself appears
      Christian rather than Judaic.

Sephore: It is quite right to follow her,
And I will do your bidding.

Joseph: Now, sir bishop, I will hurry hence,
For now a matter comes to my mind
That is necessary that I attend.

Ysakar: Farwell, Joseph and chaste Mary!
I pray God keep you together
And send you grace in kind
To serve the King of Bliss.

Mary: Father and mother, you know this situation
And how it stands with me.
I must go with my spouse
And do not know when I shall see you again.
Therefore, I pray you here in this place
For your charitable blessing,
That I shall prosper and have of you more grace*   *your continued blessing
Whatever place I be in.
On my knees before you I fall.
I pray you, dear father and mother,
Bless your own dear daughter
And pray for me in all manners,   380
As I will do for you.

Joachim: Almighty God, may He bless you,
And my blessing you also have.
God guide you in his goodness,
On land or water wherever you go.

Anne: Now God keep thee from mishaps
And protect you from all misfortune.
I pray you daughter, that you kiss me once
Before I part from you.
I pray God that He keep you safe.
I pray you, Mary, my sweet child,
Be humble and obedient, meek and mild,
Sober and discreet and never intemperate,
And you will have God's blessing.

Joachim: Farwell, Joseph, God's speed,
Whatever hall or bower you dwell in.

Joseph: May almighty God direct your ways
And keep you safe from all sorrow.

Anne: May God's grace flow to you.   400
Farewell, Mary my sweet flower!
Farewell Joseph, and God guide you.
Farewell, my child and my treasure!
Farewell my young daughter.

Mary: Farewell, dear father and mother!
Here I take my leave of you,
May God that sits in heaven bright
Have you in his keeping.

Joseph: Wife, you need to know this:
I and my kindred need to go home before you,
For truthfully, we have no house of our own.
Therefore I shall go prepare one, and then you can follow.
We are not wealthy in terms of earthly things,
And yet we will not lack for sustenance.
Meanwhile, abide here awhile, as it pleases you,
And worship your God, as makes you happy.

He that is and ever shall be,
Richest king of heaven and hell
Has chosen poverty [for us] on earth
And refused us all riches and wealth.

Mary: Go with our Lord's blessing husband.
May He speed you in all you need,
And I shall abide here until you come again,
And I will read in my Psalter.
Now, in this, blessed be our Lord
Of heaven and earth and all that bears life,
Certainly, I am most bound to You, Lord,
Now that I am both maid and wife.

Now Lord God, prepare me for prayer,
That I may say the Holy Psalms of David
Which is called the Psalter,
That I may praise Thee, my God, in so doing.
[The essence of the] virtues spoken of therein
Is that souls are lifted with what is said.
Angels are stirred to help us by this;
It lights up the darkness and drives devils away.

Psalms, the Song of Songs, is God's ditty.*   *song
Sin is driven away by it;
It teaches man to be virtuous.
It inspires man's heart spiritually.
Who that follow it* regularly,   *read/recite
[Will find that] it clarifies the heart, and fills it with charity.
He may not fail [to find] God's mercy,
That always praises God with his mouth.

O Holy Psalms! Oh, holy book!
Sweeter than any honey.
You teach them love, Lord, that look on thee
And make them desire celestial things.
With these Holy Psalms, Lord, I pray You especially
For all creatures, both the quick and the dead,   450
That You will show them your mercy
And especially to me, who reads it.
I have recited some of my Psalter, and here I am
At this Holy Psalm indeed:
"Lord you have blessed your land."
In [performing] this holy labor, Lord, help me.

Joseph: Mary, wife and most gracious maid,
I pray you are not displeased by how long I have been gone.
I have let* a pretty little house for us,   *rented
And we can quite comfortably live there.

Mary, come forth and follow me;
Now we will go to Nazareth.
And all the maidens both fair and noble,
Who attend my wife, come forth also.
Now wife, listen well to what I tell you:
I must go far from you; truly,
I must go work in a far country,
To maintain our household.
These nine months you will not see me.

Keep yourself chaste, my gentle spouse,
And all your maidens in your house,
So that I do not hear rumors roused,
For the sake of God who has all this brought about.

Mary: I pray you God's speed,
For a steadfast soul, and that he keep you
And send you resolve both night and day,
Through him be shielded and saved from all mischance.
Now, Lord of Grace, I pray to You.
Mournfully, I creep upon my knees,
Save me from sin, from pain and grief.
I mourn with my heart; I weep with my eye.
Lord God of pity,
When I sit in private contemplation,
All my heart is on Thee!
Gracious God, keep my maidenhead,
Ever pure in chastity.

The Parliament of Heaven,
Salutation & Conception

Contemplation: I say, for four thousand six hundred and four years,[20]
Man for his offense and foul folly
Has lain these years in the pains of hell
And deserved to lie there perpetually,
To perish but for your great mercy.
Good Lord have mercy on man!
Remember the prayer of Isaiah!
"Let mercy temper thy greatest might."

Then would God, who broke open the heavens with thy might,
Come down here to earth
To live there thirty-three years.
You fed your famished folk with your food,
To staunch their thirst, You let your side bleed;
Otherwise redemption would not exist.
Come visit us in this time of need!
Have compassion for your wretched creatures.

Woe to us wretches born into wretchedness!
For God has added sorrow to sorrow.
Lord, I pray You, come visit your souls!
See how they live in sin and sorrow.
Rescue your wretched creatures crying in captivity
From sorrow with thy blessed blood,
Tarry not until tomorrow, gracious Lord!
The devil has deceived them through his iniquity.

"Who shall give fountains to my eyes?" said Jeremias,
"That I must weep both day and night
To see our brethren suffer for so long."
Thy great might may rectify impiety.*   *redress mankind's sins
Lord Adam's rightful contrition is as great as the sea.
The crown has fallen from our head[s].
Man is engulfed in sin. I cry in your sight:
Gracious Lord, gracious Lord, Gracious Lord, come down!

Virtues:[21] Lord, may it please You in your high dominion,
To have pity on the man You made.
Patriarchs and prophets have made supplication.
Our office* is to offer their prayers to You: *duty

---

20 Medieval theologians calculate 4604 years between the Creation and the Nativity.
21 The play begins in heaven.

Angels, archangels, we three
That are of the first hierarchy*   *the highest position in heaven
Implore Thee, in thy high majesty, for man;
Mercy, mercy, mercy, we cry!

Lord, the angel you made so glorious,
Whose sin has made him a devil in hell,
He convinced man to rebel.
Man repented, and he [still] dwells in hell for his insurgence.
God redress his great malice
And bring man into thy grace!
Let your mercy allow him to dwell with angels
In the place that Lucifer quitted.

Father: For the wretchedness of the needy
And the lamentations of the poor,   50
I that am almighty now shall rise.[22]
The time of reconciliation has come.
My prophets have made prayers of supplication;
My contrite creatures all cry for comfort.
All my angels in heaven cry without end,
Imploring grace for man.

Truth:[23] Lord, I am thy daughter Truth.
Thy will cannot be ignored.
It would be tragic not to save your wayward creatures.

Man's offense has greatly grieved You.
When Adam sinned, You said
That he should die and go to hell.
And now restore him to bliss?
Two contraries may not dwell together.

Lord, thy truth shall last without end.
I may not turn away from Thee.
That wretch [Adam] that acted against thee
He may not have too much pain!
He vexed Thee and pleased thy foe.
You are his creator, and He is thy creature.
You have loved Truth, so it is said always.
Therefore, let him dwell forevermore in pain.

---

22   The psalm, 11:6, is first delivered by the Father in Latin.
23   The four daughters of God, allegorical personages representing the virtues—Truth, Mercy
     (Compassion), Righteousness (Justice) and Peace—debate whether God should intercede with the
     incarnation of Jesus for fallen man who is deserving of eternal punishment for Adam's Original sin.
     The debate considered divine justice and mercy to be visited through Christ's salvation.

Mercy: Oh Father of Mercy and God of Comfort
That counsels us in every tribulation [we encounter],
Let your daughter Mercy implore you
To have compassion on that man that sinned.
He is greatly sorry for his transgression.
All heaven and earth cry for mercy.
It seems to me that there should be no objection,
Since their prayers have been offered so earnestly.

Truth says she has always dwelt with Thee.
Indeed she has, as it should be.
And Thou has said Mercy shall always be reserved for man.
Then, merciful Lord, [secure] both of us[for man].
You said, "my Truth and my Mercy will be with him."
Do not let thy souls suffer and sleep in sorrow.
Order hell's hound that hates Thee to desist!
Man, no longer let the fiend keep thy love.

Righteousness [Justice]: Mercy, I marvel that you are so moved.
You know that I am your sister, Righteousness!
God is righteous, and I love righteousness!
Man offended Him forever;
Therefore, his endless punishment may never cease.
Also, he forsook his creator who made him from clay
And chose the devil as his master!
Should he be saved? No, no, no!

He would have been as wise as God?
What an abominable presumption.
It is said you know this well about me:
That the righteousness of God knows no bounds.   100
Therefore, let this be our conclusion:
He that sorely sinned, let him lie in sorrow.
Indeed, he may never atone.
Who might redeem him after this?

Mercy: Sister Righteousness! You are too vengeful!
Eternal sin, eternal God can rectify!
Above all things, God is merciful!
Though he forsook God by sin through faith, he will not forsake him ever again.
And though he never should have presumed so greatly [to become godlike],
You must consider the frailties of mankind.
Learn if it pleases you, as God teaches:
The mercy of God is endless.

Peace: It would be best to move past these divisive speeches, sisters.
Discord among the Virtues is unnatural.
The peace of God triumphs over all reason.[24]
Though Truth and Righteousness argue rationally,
Yet Mercy says what is most pleasing.
For if man's soul should abide in hell,
There will always be dissension between God and man.
And then I, Peace, could not exist [in the universe].

Therefore, it seems best to me, and you should agree,
That you should unite heaven and earth:
Put both your recommendations to our Lord.
And in his high wisdom let Him judge [which is best].
And then let us see how we shall be accorded.
It would be a pity if man's soul should perish,
Or that any one of us [Virtues] were separated from the others.

Truth: Here, in truth, I consent,
I pray our Lord to make it so.

Justice: I, Righteousness, am content,
For in Him is great equity.

Mercy: And I, Mercy, would not fly from this counsel,
I will say no more until I see what Wisdom says.

Peace: Here, now, is God; here is unity.
Heaven and earth is pleased with Peace.

Son: I think thoughts of Peace and naught of wickedness;
Thus I command you to cease arguing:
If Adam had not died, Justice would have perished,
And Truth would also have been lost.
Truth and Justice would aimlessly chase folly,
If another death did not come [my own]; Mercy would perish,
And then Peace would be exiled forever.
So two deaths must be for you four [Virtues] to be cherished.[25]

But you must know, he that shall die,
In him there can be no sin,
So that hell may have no hold on him according to God's law,

---

24 The divine will and omnipotent knowledge of God is superior to man's reason and logic. Here God's decision is also represented as a superior, supreme logic capable of resolving what may seem contrary to man.

25 This verse links Adam and Christ. The Fall of Man is the "*felix culpa*," the Fortunate Fall, which compels the coming of Christ, again moving us from Judaism to Christianity in the plays.

He must be able to leave at his liberty.*[26]

*freely

Seek out such a one, his death
Shall be the redemption for man's death.

150

Seek [you throughout] all heaven and earth,
Is this decree to your liking?

Truth: I, Truth, have sought the whole earth, within and without,
And, truthfully, to this day,
One cannot be found born without sin,
Who would not be bound to hell at death.

Mercy: I, Mercy, have travelled the whole heavenly region,
And there is none that has that much love
For man that he would suffer a deadly wound.
I cannot imagine how this should be.

Justice: Indeed, I cannot find any so worthy,
For such service none of us suffice.
His love needs to be unsurpassable,
[He] who would go to hell for man.

Peace: God is the only one who may do so.
Therefore, this is Peace's advice:
He that offered this resolution, let Him alone grant that comfort,
For in Him lies the resolution of all things.

Son: It pains me, that I made man,
That is to say, it pains me that I must suffer for him;
The Trinity must convene
And decide which of us shall restore man.

Father: Son, through your wisdom, man was made,[27]
And through wisdom, he was tempted.
Therefore through divine wisdom, you must ordain
The manner of man's salvation.

Son: Father, he that shall do this must be both God and man!
Let Me say how I may clothe Myself [in human form],
And since he was conceived through my wisdom,
I am ready to do this deed.

---

26   Refers to the Harrowing of Hell.
27   This is not a challenge to God the Father as creator of man. The idea is that God creates man through the Word, the Son, who is also wisdom. Man is tempted by the false words of the devil. Man is then saved through the true Word, Christ.

Holy Ghost: I, the Holy Ghost, will aid you two.
I will take this charge on me.
I, [who art] Love, shall lead you to your lover,
As the three of us agree, united as one.

Mercy: The lovely maid for this reconciliation is finally found!
Now we may live in peace, as it should be.
Mercy and Truth are accorded.
Justice and Pease have kissed.

    They kiss each other. *   * kiss of Peace*

Father: The good angel, Gabriel, shall be sent from us
Into the country of Galilee.
To the city known as Nazareth
To a maid who is wedded to a man
Whose name is Joseph,
And she, the noble maid
Born of the house of David, that is named
Mary, [she] shall restore all.[28]

Son: Say to her that she is without sin and full of grace,
And that I, the Son of the Godhead, shall be born by her.
Go quickly to her,
Else we shall arrive there before you.   200
I am eager to engender man there
In the meekest and purest virgin.
Say to her, she shall restore [man]
From the great Fall [to dwell] with you angels.

Holy Ghost: And if she asks how it may be [accomplished],
I shall tell her the Holy Ghost shall make it all possible.
As a sign, her barren elderly cousin Elizabeth
Is now pregnant, indeed.
Tell her, through Us, nothing is impossible.
Her body shall be filled with bliss
She shall soon find this message realized.

Gabriel: Lord, as thy emissary, I will go,
It shall be done as You wish.
Lord, behold now, I shall go:
I shall take flight and not delay.

---

28   As the Fall of Man began with woman, Eve, so now the redemption of man is made possible through woman, Mary. The concept that redemption was made possible through a woman, Mary, was one of the most significant challenges offered against antifeminist tenets, and including woman as part the salvation story was common in the late Middle Ages.

Hail [Mary], the Lord is with thee!
You are blessed among all women.
Now, the name Eve is turned to Ave.[29]
That is to say, we will no longer be filled with sorrow.

Sorrow has no place in you;
Lady, in you will be found joy.
Therefore, I add and say, "Full of grace,"
Never before was born one so full of grace.
Yet, He who has grace needs great protection.
Therefore, I say, God is with thee,
And shall keep you forever so.
You are blessed among all women!

Mary: Mercy, God! This is a marvelous message!
I am troubled by the angel's words,
I wonder what is meant by this greeting?
Angels daily appear to me,
But not in the likeness of man, as my companion,
And I am unworthy to be so highly commended.
I cannot answer,
Great shyness and dread overcome me.

Gabriel: Mary, be not afraid,
For you have found grace in God!
You shall conceive in your womb, indeed,
A child, the Son of the Trinity!
To you, his name shall be called Jesus.

He shall be great, the Son of the Highest, so called because of his nature.
And for his ancestor David, the Lord shall give him the throne,
Reigning in the house of Jacob, of whose reign there shall be no end.

Mary: Angel, I ask you,
In what way can this come to be:
For I have never [carnally] known a man.
I have always kept and will always keep my virginity.
I do not doubt the words you have said to me,
But ask how it shall be done.   250

Gabriel: The Holy Ghost shall come from above to thee,
And the virtue of Him that is the most high shall overshadow you.
Thus through the Holy Ghost you shall conceive.
He will be called the wise Son of God.

---

29   This changes the Fall through Eve into the Fortunate Fall calling forth Christ, and the "sorrow" of the
     Fall will be remedied. Ave is not related to Eve; this is folk etymology.

And see Elizabeth your cousin there?
She has conceived a son in her old age.
She is in the sixth month of her pregnancy,
Who had been called barren.
Nothing is impossible that God wills.
[In heaven,] they wait to hear your assent.

The angel waits a bit, and Mary beholds him, and the angel says:

Mary come now and make haste,
Be mindful of what you say.
[Consider] how the Holy Ghost, blessed He be,
Awaits your answer and your assent!
Through the wise action of the Divinity
Truly, the Second Person,
Will be made man incarnate
Within you, in this place.

Furthermore, take heed now
Of all the blessed spirits of virtue
That dwell in heaven before God's face,
And of all God's true and good lovers[30]
That are here in this earthly place.
Your own kin, who know the truth,
Await this time of grace, and the chosen souls
That are in hell await rescue.
Together Adam, Abraham, and David
And many others of good reputation
Desire to hear your answer.
Your assent to the Incarnation,
Will make you stand as preserver
Of all mankind's salvation![31]
Give me my answer now, Lady dear,
For all these creatures' comfort!

Mary: In all meekness, I assent to this,
Bowing my face down humbly.
So here, as handmaiden of the Lord.
Let it be done to me, according to Thy word.

Gabriel: Many thanks, my noble Lady!

---

30   Medieval texts often use the term lovers for faithful believers in God. There is nothing derogatory in
     the term. Lovers of God practice *caritas*, charitable love, which differs from *amor* which is a fleshly,
     earthly love.

31   Thus, the salvation of mankind is made dependent on a woman—Mary's consent to be the receptacle
     for Christ.

Many thanks for your answer that is celebrated on high;
Many thanks for your great humility;
Many thanks, you lantern of light.[32]

The Holy Ghost descends with three beams to our Lady. The Son of God nests within the three beams of the Holy Ghost, the good Father, and the Son, and all three enter her bosom.

Mary: Now I feel in my body
The perfect God and perfect man
Taking the bodily flesh of a child,
All at once, as God has made.

Not taking first one member* and then another,   *bodily part
But immediately the perfect body of a child,
Your handmaiden, you have now made your mother
Without pain of flesh and bone.   300
No good woman who has ever lived
Has conceived in this manner.
Oh, my Highest Father on your throne,
This is worthy of your Son, now my son, incarnate.

I cannot speak of the joy, the bliss,
That I now feel in my body.
Angel Gabriel, I thank you for this,
Most humbly recommend me to my merciful Father.
To be the Mother of God is beyond what I could imagine.
Now I will go see how my cousin Elizabeth
Has conceived, as you specified she did.
Blessed be the High Trinity!

Gabriel: Farewell turtledove, God's daughter dear,
Farwell God's mother, I honor you!
Farewell God's sister, and his companion.
Farewell, God's chamber and his bower.

Mary: Fair, gracious Gabriel.
Farewell, God's special messenger.
I thank you for great mission!
Many thanks for your great goodness,
And namely for your inspiring message,
For I understand by inspiration
What you know by special privilege
Of my son's incarnation.

---

32   Metaphor for the receptacle, for the Light-Jesus.

I pray you come often
To visit me throughout my pregnancy,
For your presence is a comfort to me.

Gabriel: So it shall be, as you wish, Lady.
[You of] gentlest blood and highest lineage
That reigns by right on earth,*   *David's descendants
As ordained by God.

I commend me to you, you throne of the Trinity!
Oh, meekest maid, now the mother of Jesus,
You are the Queen of Heaven, Lady of Earth and Empress of Hell!
Comfort[er] to all the sinful that will entreat you.
Through you body that bears the baby, our bliss shall be restored.
To you, Mother of Mercy, I humbly commend myself,
And as I began, I now end, with Ave anew,
Heaven and earth join me, and with that I ascend.

Angels sing, "Hail Mary full of grace; the Lord be with you, fair virgin."

The Annunciation to the Virgin

Joseph's Doubt[33]

Joseph: Mistress, undo the door.
Are you not home? Why have you not spoken?

Susanna: Who is there? Why do you shout so?
Tell us your errand, why have you come?

Joseph: Open the door, I say to you!
I wish to enter.

Mary: It is my spouse that speaks to us!
Open the door—his will be done.
Welcome home, my husband dear.
How have your fared in the country far away?

Joseph: Without a doubt, I have labored hard
To earn a living for you and me.

Mary: Husband, graciously we receive you home!
It truly comforts me to see you here before me.

Joseph: I marvel that I cannot see your face, surely
The sun with his beams does not shine as bright!

Mary: Husband, it is as pleases God through whom all grace grows.
Truly, whoever beholds me,
They shall be greatly stirred to virtue.
Thanks be to God for this gift and many more.

Joseph: Gentle maid, how have you fared
While I have been out of town?

Mary: Surely, sir, be not dismayed,   *as God wills
I have fared according to God's message.*

Joseph: I am afraid some evil is amiss:
Your womb stands too high!
I greatly dread that I am betrayed.
Some other man has been with thee

---

33 Joseph's concerns are briefly noted in Matthew 1:18-24. In *The Infancy Gospel of James* and some
    medieval plays, his doubts and his options are explored in more depth. This play is not considered
    part of *N-Town Mary* play, but is part of the Marion material found in that collection and worth
    attention as part of those materials known to the laity at that time.

Here while I was away.
Thy womb is great; it begins to grow!
Thou have embarked on a sinful business!
Tell me how and why
You have disgraced yourself thus!

Oh, dame, what does this mean?
You have gotten yourself great with child.
Tell me Mary, who is the child's father?
I beseech thee, tell me immediately.

Mary: The Father in Heaven and you are;
He has no other father.
Certainly, I never did sin with man.
Therefore I pray you, stay your complaint;
This child is yours and God's!

Joseph: God's child—truly, thou lies!
God never engaged so with a maid!
And I never lain with you, I dare well say,
Yet see how your womb grows!
Again Mary I ask, whose child is this?

Mary: God's and yours, I say, indeed!

Joseph: Now, all old men listen to me,
And by my advice under no circumstances   50
Wed a young lady as a wife,
For you will have doubts, and dread, and find yourself in this situation!
Alas, alas, my reputation is ruined!
All men will despise me now,
And say, "Old cuckold, this bow is bent
Just as the French say!"[34]
Alas, woe is me!
Alas, dame, why did you do this?
Because of this sin that you have done,
I forsake thee and will leave you
Once and for all!

Mary: Alas, why do you say this, good spouse?
Alas, dear husband, amend your mood!

---

34 The cuckold is a popular image in medieval tales of seduction and betrayal, most typically of an old
    husband by a young wife with a young lover. The term comes from cuckoo, and the cuckold was often
    symbolized by a horned moon, the horns—a sign of his wife's deception. The bent bow is a French
    metaphor for lechery.

It is no man, but sweet Jesus!
He will be clad in flesh and blood,
And born to your wife.

Sephore: Truly, thus the angel said,
He that is God's Son in the Trinity
Would become man for man's sake,
To save those that have been lost.

Joseph: An angel? Alas, alas, for shame!
You sin in what you say,
To so greatly blame an angel!
Alas, alas, stop, cease!
It was some boy that did this deed,
Gay and handsomely clothed,
That you now give an angel's name!
Alas, alas, and woe,
That ever this deed was done!
Ah, dame, did you think?
Here the proverb is proven true to all men:
"Though many a man beat the rushes,
Yet another man has the bird."*   *beds the woman

Mary: Gracious God in heaven's throne,
Comfort my spouse in this difficult situation!
Merciful God, take away his grief,
Since I did never gravely sin.

Joseph: Ah, sirs! What did I tell you?
That it was not to my benefit
To take a wife,
As all can well see now,
Mary is great with child,
I swear to God!
Alas, why is it so?
I will tell the bishop,
So that he may deal with her by law
And have her stoned to death!

Nay, nay, yet forbid
I could not do such a vengeful deed!
If I only knew why!   100
As God knows, I never knew her carnally,
Nor did anything that approached impropriety
In word or deed.
Notwithstanding,

Though she be meek and mild,
She could not be with child,
Without having been in the company of a man.

But I assure you, it was never me!
Though she has not done her wifely [conjugal] duty,
I will not openly complain!
Certainly, I would prefer
To leave this country forever
Than have men know of this infamy
And be rebuked by them.
And yet, many better than I
Have been made a cuckold!

Now alas, where shall I go?
I do not know what place to go to,
For oftentimes sorrow comes
And stays long before it passes.
Certainly, wife, you wronged me!
Alas, I stayed away from you too long!
All men have pity on me,
For I am sorrowful and may have no joy.

Mary: God, that possesses my body,
You know my husband is displeased
Seeing me in this plight!
He is troubled by not understanding [what has transpired];
Let him know thy perfect vision,
And thereby ease his pain.
For I would rather hold my tongue,
Bearing thy Son in secret,
As granted by the Holy Spirit,
Than reveal it myself.

God: Descend, my angel, I say
And tell Joseph
My will.
Bid him to stay and live with Mary.
For it is my Son
That she is carrying, indeed.

Angel: Almighty God of Bliss,
I am ready to go
Wherever you will me
To go, both far and wide.

Joseph, Joseph, you weep shrilly!
Why have you left your wife?

Joseph: Good sir, let me weep my fill.
Go away and let me go my way.   150

Angel: Your weeping is ill-conceived!
You act against God's will,
Change your mood and amend your thoughts!
She is a virgin!
As I tell you, she is a clean maiden, as she was before,
God willed she conceive to save mankind,
That has been lost.
Therefore I say, show her good cheer!

Joseph: Ah, Lord God, bless me!
I thank you for the comfort
That you have brought to me here.
By God, I may understand,
Such a good person as she
Would never trespass,
For she is full of grace.
I know well I misunderstood.
I will walk to my poor abode
And ask forgiveness, for I misunderstood.

Now I can plainly see,
That prophecy that was spoken
Will be proven true by this child
Who shall save mankind.
I thank you, God, that sits on high,
With heart, will and mind,
That you chose to bind me
To Mary, as my wife,
And to lead my life
So near thy glorious Son.

Alas, for joy, I quiver and quake.
What have I done?
Mercy, mercy, my gentle mate!
Mercy! I have misunderstood!
All that I have said here, I regret.
Let me now kiss your sweet feet.

Mary: Nay, do not kiss my feet.
Indeed, you can kiss my mouth
And be welcomed by me.

Joseph: Many thanks my own sweet wife.
Many thanks, my heart, my love, my life!
Never more shall I create discord
Between you and me.

Mary, Mary, may you be well
And blessed be the fruit in Thee
God's mighty Son!
Now good wife, show pity
And do not be angry with me,
Though you have good reason.
It was wrong for me
To accuse you of any sin,   200
Had you not been virtuous,
God would not be within you.

I acknowledge I have done wrong.
Certainly, I was never worthy
To be your husband.
I shall make it up to you;
Be assured, that according to your desire,
I will serve both you
And thy child hand and foot,
And worship him with great affection.
Therefore, tell me everything about the holy matter
Of your conception, and hold nothing back.

Mary: As you wish, I will as you bid me.
An angel named Gabriel came here
And greeted me and said "Ave"!
And furthermore he told me
God should be born of my body,
To vanquish the devil's power.
As I say, through the Holy Ghost,
Thus God in me does bide and dwell.

Joseph: Now I thank God with words and speech
That I was ever wedded to you, Mary.

Mary: It was the work of God, as I tell you.
Now blessed be the Lord that has chosen me.

Visit to Elizabeth

Mary: One thing I humbly pray of you:
I know that our cousin Elizabeth is with child.
If it pleases you, it would make me happy,
If we could quickly go to her, so we might comfort her.

Joseph: For God's sake! Is she with child, she?
That will make her husband Zachary glad.
As I can tell you, they dwell in the mountains far from here
In the city of Juda. I know it well, indeed.
Truly, it is fifty-two miles from here.
We will likely be weary before we come to that place.
Yet, in God's name and with good will,
We will go forth, blessed wife Mary.

Mary: Let us go, husband, though it be a hardship.
Let us go fast on this journey, I pray you,
For I am ashamed when people see me,
And fearful of them, especially men—
Pilgrims and almsgivers* who go about hastily.   *charity workers
The more the body suffers, the more the reward.
Say your devotions, and I shall say mine.
May God speed us in this journey now.

Joseph: Amen, amen, and evermore.
Dear wife, see how boldly I go forth.

They travel around the stage.

Contemplation: Sovereigns, understand that King David
Ordained that twenty-four priests of great devotion
Appear here in the temple.
They are called high priests, due to their ministrations.
And one of the high priests that has great power
Was an old priest called Zachary,
And he had a wife, an old woman of good reputation,
Called Elizabeth, who sadly never had a child.

During his service, in the hour of incensing,
The angel Gabriel appeared to him
And gave him the news that his wife should conceive.
Knowing his unworthiness and age, he did not believe it,
And a plague of muteness sealed his lips.
Then he went home and saw his wife was pregnant.

Gabriel also told our Lady of this conception,
And truly, soon after, Mary sought the sage woman.

Here is the story
Of the meeting of the two;
God bless our endeavor,
And I will cease speaking.

Joseph: Ah wife, truly, I am weary.
Therefore, I will sit down and rest myself here.
See wife, here is the house of Zachary.
If you wish, I will call Elizabeth to come out to you.

Mary: No husband, if it pleases you, I shall go to her.
Now the blessed Trinity be in this house!
Ah, cousin Elizabeth, sweet mother, how are you?
You grow great with child! My God, you are beautiful!   50

Elizabeth: As soon as I heard your holy greeting,
Humble maiden and Mother of God, Mary,
The Holy Ghost, by his breath, inspired us.
The child in my body rejoiced greatly,
And reverently knelt down on his knees to our God,
Who you bear in your body, as I truly know!
Filled with the Holy Ghost, thus loudly I exclaim:
Blessed are thou among women!
And blessed is the fruit of thy womb, as well.

How is it that the worthiest virgin and wife that ever was created,
The Mother of God, should come to me,
Wretch of wretches, a creature worse than all?
And they are blessed that believe in the miracle
The word of God engendered in thee.
How this blessedness was brought about,
I cannot imagine or say how that it came to pass.

Mary: It can be said that it was for the praise of God, cousin.
While I sat in my little house, praying to God,
Gabriel came and said to me, "Ave!"
When I consented, I conceived God,
Perfect God and perfect man became at once [one within me].
Then the angel said to me,
That it was six months since you had conceived.
This is why I have come here, to see and to comfort you, cousin.

Elizabeth: Blessed be you for coming here, cousin.
How I conceived, I shall tell you:
The angel appeared to me at the hour of incensing,
Saying I should conceive, and [Zachary] thought it could not be.
Truly, for his disbelief, he has been mute since then.
And now I have told you something of my conception.

Mary: With this holy psalm, I begin today:[35]
My soul praises my Lord,
And my soul rejoices in God—my salvation.

Elizabeth: With joy, by the Holy Ghost, God's Son comes through you.
Let your spirit rejoice that God has so visited you.

Mary: Because He has so regarded the humility of his handmaid,
From this time forward all generations will call me blessed.

Elizabeth: For He beheld the humility of you, his handmaid,
Henceforth, all generation will be blessed through you.

Mary: And his mercy is from generation to generations,
To those fearing him.

Elizabeth: Yes, his mercy is from that generation into the generation of peace,
Now He comes to all that fear Him.

Mary: Because He who is mighty has done great things for me,
And holy is his name.

Elizabeth: Great and mighty things He has made,
And his name is greatly worshipped by us.

Mary: Through the power of his arm
He has scattered the proud of imagination by his heart.

Elizabeth: With the power in his right arm He has made   100
The proud despair, through the thoughts* of their hearts alone.   *doubts

Mary: He pulled the mighty down from their thrones
And exulted the meek.

Elizabeth: He pulled the proud men down from their high seats,
And places the meek upon the high seats of peace.

---

35 The exchange that follows echoes Luke 1:46-55. Mary speaks the Latin scripture, and Elizabeth then
    repeats and translates it into the vernacular, English.

Mary: He has filled the hungry with good [sustenance]
And sent the rich away empty.

Elizabeth: All the poor and needy He fills with his good [sustenance],
And He lets the rich fall into nothingness.

Mary: He has received his servant Israel,
That remembered his mercy.

Elizabeth: He took up his child, Israel, that came to Him
Remembering his mercy, for these are his.

Mary: As He spoke to our fathers,
To Abraham and his seed for always.

Elizabeth: As He spoke here to our forefathers in secret,
Abraham and also all those of his seed in this world.

Mary: Glory be to the Father and the Son
And the Holy Spirit.

Elizabeth: Praise be to the Father in heaven,
The same to the Son, here as well,
And acknowledgement of the Holy Ghost, too.

Mary: As it was in the beginning and now and forever,
And into the age of ages, amen.

Elizabeth: As it was in the beginning, and now is and forever shall be,
And in this world, in all good works performed therein.

Mary: This psalm of divine inspiration is recited between the two of us.
In heaven, it is written with angel's hand
Ever to be sung and also read
Everyday at evensong* by us.[36]   *vespers/evening prayers

Now, cousin Elizabeth, I shall stay here with you
And abide these three months.
To help you wash, scour, and sweep till you have your child,
In all this, I can be of aid to you.

Elizabeth: You Mother of God, you show us, who are wretches,
How we should be humble.

---

36   This exchange asserts that women could both be taught and speak Scripture.

All heaven and earth worship you
That is the throne and tabernacle of the High Trinity!

Joseph: How are you? How are you doing, Zachary?
Without a doubt, old age is upon us.
Why do you shake your head so? Do you suffer from a palsy?
Why don't you speak? Certainly you are not angry.

Elizabeth: Nay, wise father Joseph, it is not because he is unwilling.
It is a visitation* from God that he may not speak.   *punishment
Therefore, let us both thank God, [and pray]
That through his mercy, He shall remedy it when it pleases Him.

Come, I entreat you,
For certainly you are welcome, Mary,
For your most comforting visit, thanks be to God.[37]

Contemplation: Listen people, here is the conclusion: 150
How the Ave was made, here we have been taught.
The angel said: "Hail, full of grace, the Lord is with thee,
Blessed are thou among women."
Elizabeth said, "And blessed
Is the fruit of thy womb." Thus the church added "Mary" and "Jesus" here.
Who says our Lady's psalter for a year,
Will have pardon ten thousand and eight hundred years.[38]

To speak of how things progressed,
As we read, Mary dwelt there
With Elizabeth for three full months,
Thanking God with her whole heart.

Lord God, what a house this was
With these children and their two mothers
Mary and Elizabeth, Jesus and John,
And Joseph and Zachary, also!

And our lady dwelt there
Till John was born of his mother.
And indeed, then Zachary spoke,
Who had been mute and lost his ability to speak.

---

37   In some cases, the play would end at this point, without Contemplation reentering to summarize the events that were to be skipped over.

38   Years reduced from the time need to be spent in purgatory to pay for one's sins.

He and Elizabeth offered up prayers to God:
They blessed the Lord
And offered praise and blessings.
They immediately offered these devotions.

When that was done, after this,
Our noble lady took her leave
Of Elizabeth and Zachary
And kissed John and blessed him.

Now, most humbly, we thank you for your patience
And beseech you for your support.
If anything we have done here offends,
We ask that you forgive it, as that was not our intent.
We beseech Christ's precious Passion
To keep and protect you, and reward you for coming here.
With Ave we begun and with Ave we conclude:
"Hail queen of heaven" to Our Lady we sing.

The Trial of Mary and Joseph[39]

Den (a summoner):[40] Clear the way, sirs, and let my lord bishop come
And preside over the court, and enforce the laws.
And I shall precede them to that place and summon them!
Those that are in my book, you must come to the court.

I advise you here about
That I can summon all of you!
Look that you do not fail
To appear at court:
Both John Jordon and Geoffrey Guile,[41]
Malkin Milkduck and fair Mable,
Steven Sturdy and Jack-at-the-Stile,
And Sauder Saddler,

Tom Tinder and Beatrice Belle,
Pier Potter and What-at-the-Well,
Sim Smallfaith and Kate Kell,
And Bartholomew the Butcher,
Kit Cackler and Colette Crane,
Gil Fetish and Fair Jane,
Paul Pewterer and Pernel Prawn,
And Phillip the good Fletcher.

Cook Crane and Davy Drydust,
Lucy Liar and Leticia Little Trust,
Miles the Miller and Cole Crack Crust,
Both Betty the Baker and Robin the Red,
And look that you dig deep in your purse,

39   Where the Jewish priests and bishops have been shown in an unbending, yet fair light before, in this
     play the ecclesiastic court—the court of the Church which presides, judges, and sentences individuals
     for their sins and infractions against the Church—is shown in a more negative light, particularly
     through the people it employs such as the summoner, Den, and the detractors. They represent the
     corrupt influences employed by the Church in the High Middle Ages. The bishop, Abiathar, like
     Ysakar, is represented as stern and fair, but surrounded by these questionable figures of corruption.

40   A summoner delivered summons to people to appear before the ecclesiastic court for infractions
     against the Catholic Church during the Middle Ages. The accusations were "recorded in his book"
     which he then announced/read to the accused.

41   This is intended to be a list of common names and occupations that could be found in any locale and
     that could be summoned to the ecclesiastic court for committing a variety of sins such as blasphemy,
     gossiping, petty theft, adultery etc. The summoner suggests every location is full of such types.

Or else you will have cause to fear the worse (punishment from the court),[42]
Though you sling God's curse
At my head,
Come quickly.
Both Booting the Brewster and Sibyl Sling,
Meg Merryweather and Sabin Spring,
Tiffany Twinkler, do not fail for anything!
Court is this day.

Here begins the trial of Mary and Joseph. The first detractor says:

Detractor 1 (Raise-Slander): Ah, sirs, God save you all!
In faith, here is a good company.
Good sirs, tell me what men call me—
I believe you would not (do so) on this day,
Though I walk far and wide.
For where I come, I do no good,
Raising slander is my vocation.
Backbiter is my brother by blood.

I wish he would come here today.
I wish to God that he were here.
And by my truth, I dare well say,
That if we two appear together,
The two of us shall raise more slander
Within an hour throughout this town
Than ever there was this [past] thousand years,
Or else I would curse you both up and down.

Now, by my truth, I can see   50
My brother; here he is.
Welcome, dear brother, I swear my alliance to you,
Let me now kiss your gentle mouth.[43]

Detractor 2: Greetings brother, I am happy too.
I am glad we meet this day.

---

42   Summoners often collected fines in lieu of the accused appearing before the court and pocketing
      the money for themselves. Many also made up false charges, supposedly reading them off of bills
      in their "book," to individuals who could not read (and even if they could, they would not be able
      to read the Latin they would be written in). The accused had to naively assume the summoner was
      acting in good faith as an officer of the Church. The summoner would assure them that if they paid
      him, he would make sure the summons was discharged, and they would not have to go before the
      ecclesiastic court to answer the charges. See for example, "The Friar's Tale," in *The Canterbury Tales*,
      by Geoffrey Chaucer. Of course, if the charge did not exist, the individual had been dubbed and had
      nothing to worry about from the court. If it were a valid accusation made by the court, a simple fee
      would generally not be conditions of the sentence to prove contrition and penance. Furthermore,
      summoners were not empowered to pass judgment or collect restitution.
43   Parody of the kiss of peace.

Detractor 1: Right so am I brother, indeed.
More glad than I can say.
But yet, good brother, I pray you,
Tell all the people your name,
For if they knew it, I bet my life,
They would worship you and speak of your fame.

Detractor 2: I am Backbiter, both recognized
And known in many places, [as he] that ruins all happiness,

Detractor 1: By my truth, I said the same,
And some wished you [would fall on] bad luck.

Detractor 2: Hark, Raise-slander, have you any news
Of any thing that has been done lately?

Detractor1: A short time ago, a thing happened.
I believe you will have a good laugh at it,
For truly, if it be known,
Great hate will come of it.

Detractor 2: If I may raise dissension by it,
I will not wait to sow the seed of slander.

Detractor 1: Sir, true to say, in the temple,
There was a maid called Mary.
She appeared to be very holy.
Men say she was fed by a holy angel.
She made a vow to never lie with man,
But to always live as a chaste and clean virgin.
However, it has come to pass, that her womb swells
And is as great as yours or mine!

Detractor 2: Yes, I swear, that old rascal Joseph—
Was so enamored with that maid,
When he had sight of her beauty,
He pursued her until he had her abed.

Detractor 1: No, no, she has paid him back poorly [for treating her well].
She has well loved some fresh young gallant
That has lain with her,
And that sorely grieves the old man.

Detractor 1: By my truth, that may well be,
For she is fresh and fair to behold,

And it seems to me, such a morsel
Would delight a young man.

Detractor 1: Such a bright, beautiful young damsel.
Such a nice figure
And lascivious tail[44]
Would be titillating under you.

Detractor 2: That old cuckold was cruelly beguiled
By the fresh wench when he wedded her.
Now he must father another man's child   100
And raise it with his labor.*   *support/provide for

Detractor 1: A young man gives more pleasure in bed
To a young wench than an old one.
That is the reason this so often happens
And many a man is cuckolded.

Abiathar enters between two doctors of the law. He hears the accusation, calls the detractors, and he says,

Bishop Abiathar: Harken, fellows! Why speak you such shame
Of that good virgin, Maid Mary?
You are accursed who defame her so!
You make many a heart heavy
By speaking such villainy
Of she that lives such a good and holy life.
I charge you to cease your false outcry,
For she is a kinswoman of my own blood.

Detractor 2: Though she be your kinswoman,
Her womb swells great with child!
Do call her here. See for yourself,
That what I tell you is the truth.

Detractor 1: Sir, for your sake I shall hold my tongue,
I loathe to cause you grief,
But listen sires to what is rumored—
Our fair maid is now great with child.

Doctor of the Law 1: Take care what you say sir.
Be sure of what you present.
If this be found to be false on another day,
You will be sorry to have to repent your story.

---

44   Detractor 1 is making a crude reference to her sexual parts and inferring that they lure young men.

Detractor 2: Sir, truly, the maid is good and attractive,
Both pretty and gay, and she is a fair maid,
And slyly, with help, she consented
To make her husband a cuckold.

Doctor of Law 2: Watch your tongue!
I hope to God you prove false!
It would be a great pity if she so offended
By any such wrongdoing.

Bishop Abiathar: These are heavy tales. It grieves my heart
To hear such foul speech about her.
If she is found blameworthy,
She shall sorely rue her behavior.

Summoner, in haste go your way!
Tell Joseph and his wife by name
To appear at court this day,
To purge her of this defamation.*   *to answer the charge
Say that I hear great shame spoken of her
And that causes me great heaviness.
If they are clean and without blame,
Bid them come here and bear witness.

Den: All right, sir, I shall summon them.
To appear here at your court.
And if I can find them, as I hope,
They shall soon be here.
Away, sirs, let me come near!   150
I, a man of worship, come here.
You seem to need to be taught how to be courteous!
Take off your hoods![45] Curse you!
Give me coin[46]
Or by my faith,
I shall summon you,
And for fear you, will quake in your shoes!
But if you fill my purse,
I will retract my accusations.
Gold or silver, I will take,
As every summoner will.

---

45 The doctors of ecclesiastic law wear hoods; in the present day, these are the hoods ceremonially granted to Ph.D.s when earning their doctorates. The doctors treat the summoner with disdain, seeming to know of his reputation.

46 He invites them to pay him off.

Good day Joseph, to you and your fair spouse.
My lord, the bishop has sent for you.
He has told me that in your house
A cuckold dwells every night.
He [that is] so treated is likely to be ruined.
Fair maid, you can best tell what happened.
Now, truly, tell your version,
Did not some young gallant please you well?

Mary: God is my witness:
That sinful work was never in my thought.
I am still as pure a virgin,
As I was when I was born into this world.

Den: Other witnesses are not needed.
You are with child, as every man can see.
I charge you both, do not tarry,
But come with me to the bishop.

Joseph: We will go to the bishop with you;
We have no doubt that we will be exculpated.

Mary: Almighty God shall be our friend,
When the truth is discovered!

Den: Thus every wanton woman protests
When her sin is revealed.
But men begin to yield
When they are guilty and found blameworthy.

Therefore, come forth, cuckold by name,
The bishop will examine your life.
Come forth, you too good dame,
A pure wife, as I suppose.
I shall tell you, without pleasantries,
If you were mine, without fail,
I would curse you everyday,
If you brought me a baby.

My lord the bishop, I have brought here
This good couple at your bidding,
And as judged by me, by her burden,
She will soon sing a "fair child, lullaby."

Detractor 1: If you brought her a cradle,
You might save her money.*   *a fine by the court

As she is your young kinswoman.
Sir, I pray you that worse never befall her.

Bishop: Alas Mary! What have you done?
I am ashamed, for your sake!
Why have you abandoned your holy ways?
Did old Joseph overcome you,
Or have you chosen another mate
Who has brought you to shame?
Tell me, who has done this villainy?
How have you lost your holy name?

Mary: I hope my name is safe and sound.
As God has witnessed, I am a virgin!
I have never succumbed to lascivious thought
Or fleshly lust in thought or deed.

Doctor of Law 1: How should your womb rise then?
It is greatly swollen—
Other than if you had laid with some man?
Otherwise your womb should never be so great, indeed.

Doctor of Law 2: Hark Joseph, I am afraid
That you have worked this open sin!
You have betrayed this woman
With great flattery and sinful play.

Detractor 2: You have uncovered his ploy,*   *how he seduced her
I definitely agree that is how it was.
Now tell us how you won her over
Otherwise make it known that you are a cuckold!

Joseph: To me, she is a true clean maid,
And I, for her, am also clean.
I have never tried to lead her into fleshly sin,
Since she has wedded me.

Bishop: You shall not escape from us just now:
First, you shall tell us another tale.
Straight to the altar you shall go,
And be tested by the drink of vengeance.[47]
Here is the bottle of God's judgment;
This drink shall now be your purgation.
It has such power by God's ordinance

---

47   This is trial by ordeal: God is seen to pass judgment for the community by determining if the accused
     should live or die by whether s/he survives drinking the potion.

That whatever man drinks of this potion,
And certainly, if he circles*   *makes procession about
The altar, in this place—
If he is guilty of any sin,
His face shall openly show it.

If you be guilty, tell us, let us see,
Our God's might is not to be underestimated.
If you are guilty,
You will aggrieve God many times over.

Joseph: I am not guilty, as I first told you.
Almighty God is my witness.

Bishop: Then quickly drink this potion you hold,
And prepare to make a procession round the altar.

Joseph drinks and circles the altar seven times saying:

Joseph: I take this drink with the intent of proving   250
I am guiltless to God. I pray,
Lord, as You are omnipotent,
Show the truth in me this day.

He drinks.

I make my way around this altar.
Oh gracious God, help thy servant,
Since, I am guiltless against You,
May your hand of mercy grant my prayer.

Den: This old rascal can barely move!
He takes his time going around.
Lift up your feet! Set forth your toes.
Or by my faith, you will be beaten!

Detractor 1: Now sir, bad luck smacks you in the face!
What afflicts your legs so that they now are lame?
They served you well
When you played with yonder young lady!

Detractor 2: I pray God give him bad luck!
Your legs give way under you, old man.
But when he danced* with this damsel   *had sex
He had plenty of vigor!

Den: Then the rascal was aroused,
And at the time [he] lusted to play.
Did she not give you a hot drink
To comfort your addled brain?

Joseph: Gracious God! Help me against these people
That defame me at this time;
I have never touched her body.
This day help me circle about this altar
To keep my reputation from worldly shame.
Seven times I have gone round about,
If I deserve to suffer blame,
Oh rightful God, then show my sin openly!

Bishop: Joseph, heartily thank God, thy Lord,
Who in his high mercy does exculpate you,
Offering proof of your innocence, as we will record,
That you never sinned with her.
Now Mary, you may not refuse [the potion]
Though we see you stand here great with child.
What mystery man abused you?
Why have you sinned against thy husband?

Mary: I never trespassed with any earthly creature;
Therefore, I hope through God's dispensation
To be proven innocent of all sin
Like my husband, in your sight.
I take the bottle out of your hand.
Here, I shall drink before you,
And submit to circling the altar
Seven times, by God's grace.

Doctor of Law 1: See how this bold wretch presumes,
Daring God to prove his might!
Though God's vengeance will consume her,   300
She shall not admit her villainy!
You are with child; we see it!
Your womb accuses you!
There was never any woman in such a plight
Whose behavior could excuse her.

Detractor 1: Truly, I suppose that this woman slept
Without covers while it snowed

And a flake crept into her mouth
And thereafter a child grew in her womb![48]

Detractor 2: Beware woman, for this is well known:
I believe, when it is born,
If the sun shines, it will turn into water again,
For snow always turns again to water.

Doctor of Law 2: I advise you, by God,
Look that you do take this trial lightly.

If you be guilty, you will not escape.
Always fear God, that rightful justice.
If God in his vengeance judges you,
Not only you but all your kindred will be shamed.
Better to tell the truth completely
Than to grieve God and be punished by Him.

Mary: I trust in his grace; I shall never grieve Him.
I am his servant in word, deed and thought.
I hope to prove myself a maiden undefiled.
I pray you, do not hinder me.

Bishop: Now this I say, if the good Lord our God
That has made all this world sends any kind of sign
As proof against you, if his vengeance is visited on you,
It will be very costly.

Hold the bottle and take a large drink
And proceed to circle the altar.

Mary: I have entrusted my case to God.
Lord, with your help, I drink this potion.

The Blessed Virgin drinks the potion and afterwards circles the altar, saying:

God, I have never been defiled by man
But have always lived a true virgin.
Send me this day your holy consolation
So that all these fair people can see [proof of] my purity!

O gracious God, since You have chosen me
To be thy mother by which You will be born,

---

48   Their attack ironically alludes to the idea of virginal conception. It is also interesting to note that this
     idea of incarnation echoes the lyric "I sing of a maiden" and found in sermons and commentaries
     from that period.

Save your tabernacle that is kept chaste for You,
Who is now reproached and scorned.
Before You came, Gabriel told me with words,
That You would make me with child.
Help me now through your majesty so that my reputation is not ruined.
Dear Son, I pray You, help your humble mother!

Bishop: Almighty God, what does this mean?
Despite all God's potion that she has drank
This woman with child remains fair and clean
Without any foul spot or sign!
I cannot by any stretch of the imagination   350
Judge her guilty or sinful!
It is shown openly by exculpation:
She is a clean maid, both mother and wife!

Detractor 1: By my father's soul, there is great guile here!
Because she is one of your kindred,
The drink has been changed by some trickery,
So she would not be defamed at this time.

Bishop: Because you deem that we commit falsehoods,
And since you defamed them first,
Despite what you want, you shall
Drink the same before all the people here.

Detractor 1: In good faith, sir, I'll take one drink,
If these two drinkers have not emptied it.

Here he drinks, and feeling a pain in his head, falls and says:

Ow, out! What is this pain in my skull?
My head burns with fire!
Mercy, good Mary! I do repent
My cursed and false accusation.

Mary: Now, good Lord in heaven, omnipotent,
Of his great mercy, assuage your sickness.

Bishop: We all fall on our knees here on the ground.
Praying you, God's handmaiden for grace.
Good Mary, forgive us here in this place,
For all the cursed language and defaming words.

Mary: Now God forgive you all your trespass,
And also forgive you all the defamation
You uttered, more and less,
To slander and defile me.

Bishop: Now blessed virgin, we all thank you
For your good heart and great patience.
We will go home with you
To serve you with high reverence.

Mary: I thank you heartily for your benevolence.
Go home to your own house, I pray you,
And take these people home with you hence.
I am not prepared to leave here.

Bishop: Then farewell, maid and pure virgin.
Farewell, true handmaid of God in bliss.
We all bow to you
And take leave of you who is most worthy.

Mary: Almighty God, your ways are wise,
For You, high Lord, are most mighty.
May He guide you so that you may not miss
Having sight of Him in heaven.

Joseph: The high Lord in heaven be honored,
Whose endless grace is so abundant.
That He does show the truth
To each creature that is his true servant.
In this place, we both are bound
To worship that Lord with joyful heart
Who granted our exculpation   400
And proved us pure, by his high grace.

Mary: Truly, good spouse, I greatly thank Him
For his good grace in exonerating us.
Our purity is openly known
By virtue of his great solace.

   It joyfully ends here.

The Nativity

THE VIRGIN MARY AND MARY MAGDALENE IN THE DRAMA OF LATE MEDIEVAL ENGLAND

The Nativity

Joseph: Lord, what hardship befalls man!
There is no rest in the world for him!
Octavian, our emperor, has firmly demanded
That we bring him tribute: everyone must go forth.
It is proclaimed in every borough and city by name.
I that am but a poor carpenter,
Born of the blood of David,
I must obey the emperor's commandment
Or else I would be blameworthy.

Now, my wife, Mary, what do you say to this?
Indeed, I must go forth
To the city of Bethlehem.
Certainly, I must will my body to do this deed.

Mary: My husband, and my spouse, I will go with you,
I would gladly see that city.
If I might find any of my family there,
It would be a great joy to me.

Joseph: My spouse, you are with child; I fear for you traveling.
It seems an unwise undertaking to me.
But I will gladly do as you please,
Since women are easily irritated when they are with child.

Now let us go forth as fast as we can,
And Almighty God speed us on our journey.

Mary: My sweet husband, would you tell me
What tree that is standing other there on the hill?

Joseph: Truly, Mary, it is called a cherry tree,
In season, you could eat of it until you were full.

Mary: Turn again husband and behold yonder tree,
See how it blooms so sweetly.

Joseph: Come on, Mary, it is time that we were in the city,
Or else we will be in trouble, I tell you truly.

Mary: Now, my spouse, behold I pray you
How the cherries grow upon yonder tree,[49]
I would gladly have some.
If it would please you to fetch some for me.

Joseph: Your desire for fruit I shall certainly appease,[50]
Ow! It is hard work to pluck these cherries.
For the tree is so high that picking them will not be easy.
Therefore, let Him pluck the cherries who got you with child!

Mary: Now, good Lord, I pray You, grant me this boon,
To have these cherries, if it is your will.
Now I thank You, God: this tree bows down to me.
I may now gather enough and eat my fill.

Joseph: Ow! I know well I have offended my God in Trinity,
Speaking these unkind words to my spouse,
Now, I believe it cannot other be otherwise,
But that my spouse bears the King's Son of Bliss.
He helps us now in our need.
Of the kin of Jesse, worthily you are born:
Kings and patriarchs went before you.   50
All these worthy men were your kindred,
As clerks tell in histories.

Mary: Many thanks for what you have said.
Let us wisely go forth.
The Almighty Father is our comfort;
The glorious Holy Ghost is our friend.

Joseph: Hail, worshipful sir, and good day.
You seem to be a citizen of this city.
I ask you for a lodging for my spouse and me.

For truly, this woman is very weary
And would be glad of rest, sir.
We have come to this city
To fulfill the bidding of our emperor
To pay tribute, as is our duty,
And to keep ourselves from misfortune [resulting from failing to obey the edict].

---

49 The English Cherry Tree Carol derives from this incident. The appearance of the fruit in the midst
    of winter highlights the miraculous fecundity of the virgin. The cherry fruit is round, symbolizing
    perfection without beginning or end, and the red color symbolizes martyrdom—hence Jesus.
50 This is a pun on the concept of sexual appetite, often found in tales of adultery and cuckoldry. Here,
    the appetite is the virgin's in antithetical to that idea, and the fruit's appearance miraculous.

Citizen: Sir, I know of no inn in this town
That your wife and you can sleep in.
The city is beset with people everywhere,
[So that] they [even] lie outside on the streets.

No man can find a dwelling place now.
Once you are within the city gate,
Without a doubt, scarcely a place can be found
Even on the street to rest.

Joseph: Nay, sir I will not debate this!
Such things are beyond my power
But all my care and thought
Is for Mary, my darling dear.

Ah, sweet wife, what shall we do?
Where shall we lodge this night?
We pray to the Father of Heaven
To keep us [safe] from every wicked creature.

Citizen: Good man, one more word I will say to you,
If you will do as I counsel.
Yonder a stable stands by the way,
Among the beasts you may find lodging.

Mary: Now the Father in heaven reward you.
His son is in my womb, truly He is.
He will keep you and protect you everywhere.
It is now time for us to go hence husband.

Hark, good husband, I know right well
A new revelation is made to me:
Christ who in me has taken incarnation,
Truly, I know will soon be born.

Here, in this poor lodging I will take shelter,
To await the blessed birth
Of Him that made all this world.
Between my sides, I feel Him stir!

Joseph: God help you, spouse, it greatly grieves me,
God's son shall be born, among beasts
In this feeble and lowly lodging.   100
Yet, his wondrous works must be fulfilled,

In this barren house, without any walls,
Here, [where there] is no fire or wood.

Mary: Joseph, my husband, I will abide here,
Here the King's Son of Bliss will be born.

Joseph: Now, gentle wife, be of good cheer,
And tell me what you think you need.
I shall get it, whether it be plentiful or scarce,
Tell me what food and drink you desire.

Mary: I have no desire for food or drink:
Almighty God shall be my food.
Now that I have come within the stable,
I hope to see my child.
Therefore husband, out of decency,
Leave this place, quickly,
And alone in humility
I shall await God's high grace.

Joseph: All right, wife, I will do as you please
And leave this place
And seek some midwives to help you
When you go into labor this day.
Farewell true wife and clean maid,
God in the Trinity be your comfort.

Mary: I pray to God in heaven for you—
He will preserve you wherever you go.

While Joseph is gone, Mary bears the Only Begotten Son.

Joseph: Now God, from whom all relief comes,
And as all grace is grounded in You,
Save my wife from hurt and pain,
Till I can find some midwives to attend her.
Women in labor suffer great pains
While they cry out.
God help my wife so that she does not swoon*—   *faint
I am very sorry she is alone.

It is not proper for a man to be
There when a woman goes into labor!
Therefore I must seek some midwife
To help my wife that is so young.

Zelomy: Man, why do you moan so?
Tell me something about your grief.

Joseph: My wife is in great distress.
[She is] now in labor and all alone.
For God's love that sits in the throne,
As you are midwives that can greatly
Help my young wife, hasten at once!
I fear for that young woman.

Salome: Be of good cheer and of glad mood—
We two midwives will go with you.
Never a woman stood in such plight
That we were not ready to aid [her].

My name is Salome. All men know me   150
As a midwife of good repute.
When women are in labor, grace grows.
There I come, I have never failed [to do so].

Zelomy: And I am Zelomy; men know my name.
We two will go together with you
And help your wife and keep her from harm.
Come forth, Joseph, we will go there straightaway.

Joseph: I thank you dames; you comfort me.
We will go straight away to my wife,
Where in a poor lodging lies Mary.
Try to comfort her, my friends.

Salome: Truly, we cannot enter the dwelling!
There is therein so great brightness—
Moon by night or sun by day
Shone never so clear in their lightness.

Zelomy: I dare not go into this house!
The wonderful light frightens me!

Joseph: Then I will go in alone by myself
And comfort my wife, if I may.
All hail, wife and maiden, I say!
How are you doing? Tell me how you fare.
I have brought two good midwives.
To comfort you in your childbed this day,

To help you in your hard labor—
Zelomy and Salome have come with me.
But out of dread of the bright light
That they see, they stand outside and dare not enter.

Here, Mary smiling, says:

Mary: The might of Godhead in his majesty
Will not be hidden at this time.
The child that is born will prove his mother free of sin,[51]
A very clean maid, and therefore I smile.

Joseph: Why do you laugh wife?[52] That is disgraceful!
I pray you to stop doing this, spouse!
Perhaps it will offend the midwives,
And then they will not help you in your time of need.
If you have need of midwives,
It would be unfortunate, if they went away.
Therefore be somber, if you can,
And grateful for the midwives' attention.

Mary: Husband, I pray you, don't be displeased
That I laugh and have great joy,
Here the child that made this world
Is born now of me, He who shall save everything.

Joseph: I ask your grace, for I was raving.
O gracious child, I ask mercy—
As you are Lord and I am but a peasant
Forgive me now for my banality!

Alas midwives, what have I said?
I pray you, come closer.
Here I find my wife, a maid,   200
And in her arm here, she has a child!
She is at the same time, both maid and mother.
That which God wills never fails to pass.
There has never been a mother on earth so pure
[If she were not], she would have suffered labor pains.

---

51   Free of Original Sin, hence she has not suffered the pains of childbirth.
52   This is divine laughter and different than common laughter. Divine laughter uttered by characters in literature shows their transcendence of earthly concerns and awareness of their transitory nature and is a celebration of divine grace and eternal bliss.

Zelomy: She must suffer labor pains in birth
Or else no child could be born of her!

Joseph: I pray you dame, and ye can vouchsafe*—   *see/test for yourself
Come see the child my wife bore.

Salome: Great God in this place!
Sweet sister, how are you doing?

Mary: I thank the Father of his high grace.
That you can see his own Son and my child here.

Zelomy: Hail Mary and good morning!
Who was the midwife for this fair child?

Mary: He that will never abandon anyone
Sent me this babe, and I am a pure maid.

Zelomy: Let me touch and feel with my hand
To see if you need medicine.
I will aid and comfort you well,
If you are in pain, as I have helped other women.

Mary: From this blissful birth of mine
I have had neither pain nor grief.
I am a clean maid and pure virgin.
Feel with your hand yourself.

Zelomy touches Mary.

Zelomy: Oh mighty God, have mercy on me!
This is a miracle never heard of before!
Here openly I feel and see
A fair child is born of a maiden.
And she needs no cleansing as others do,
Full clean and pure He truly came,
Without spot or any pollution,
Of his mother, whose virginity is intact.[53]

Come near, good sister Salome:
Behold the breasts of this clean maid,
And how they are full of fair milk,
And her clean child, as I can attest—

---

53 The midwives test to see that Mary's hymen is intact. The cleanness meaning there is no afterbirth or
    blood (pollution). This and the lack of labor pains is proof, attested to by the midwives, that not only
    are Mary and the child pure but that Jesus is born without Original Sin.

Clean and pure, both mother and child!
I am baffled by this matter,
Seeing them both unstained.

Salome: It is not true! It may never be
That both are clean! I cannot believe—
A maid has milk! No man has ever seen
A woman bear a child without undergoing labor pains.
I will never believe it, unless I test for myself,
By examining her with my hand.
In good conscience, I can never accept
That she has a child and is still a maid.

Mary: To put an end to your doubts,   250
Touch me with your hand
Thoroughly examine me and attest to the truth,
Whether I am unclean or a pure maiden.

Salome touches and examines Mary with her hand, howling and weeping:

Salome: Alas, alas,
For my great doubt and lack of faith!
My hand is dead and dry as clay!
My distrust has brought me misfortune!
Alas the time that I was born,
Since I have offended against God's might!
My hand's power is now all gone—
Stiff as a stick and may not move,
For I did test this bright maid
And contested her pure cleanness!
Now I am afflicted with great misfortune.
Alas, alas for my wickedness!

Oh Lord of Might, You know the truth,
That I have always dreaded You.
I have taken pity on every poor creature
And given them alms for love of Thee,
Both wife and widow that asked in your name,
And friendless children that had great need,
I cared for them, all for You,
And took no money or reward.

Now I am a wretch, who did not believe,
As I showed by insisting on testing this maid;
My hand is dead and grieves me.
Alas, that I ever examined her!

Angel: Women, this sorrow that assuages you—
Worship that child that was born there,
Touch the cloth that He is laid in,
And He shall restore all that was lost.

Salome: O glorious child and King of Bliss:
I ask your mercy for my trespass.
I know I sinned; I judged wrongly.
O blessed babe, grant me some grace:
[And] Of you maid, [who is] also here in this place,
Kneeling on my knee, I ask mercy.
Most holy maid, grant me solace—
Say some word of comfort to me.

Mary: As God's angel told you,
My child is medicine for every illness;
Touch his clothes, by my counsel—
He will quickly restore your hand.

Salome touches the hem of Christ's gown:

Salome: Now blessed be this child forever!
He is truly the Son of God,
He has healed my hand that was lost
Through lack of faith and bad judgment.

I will proclaim in every place:
That God is born of a clean maid,
And in our likeness God is now clad   300
To save mankind that has been lost.
His mother is a maid, as she was before,
Not foul or polluted, as other woman be.

She is fair and fresh, as a rose on the thorn,
Lily-white, clean in pure virginity.
Of this blessed babe I now take my leave
And you too, high Mother of Bliss.
Truly, I shall go tell in every place,
Of this great miracle that I have witnessed.

Mary: Farewell, good dame, and God guide you on your way.
May God send you prosperity in all your journeying,
And in his high mercy may the Lord so bless you
That you never more offend in word, thought or deed.

Zelomy: And I also take my leave
Of all this blessed good company
Praying for your grace on us both far and near,
Grant us your endless mercy.

Joseph: The blessing of the Lord that is most mighty
Go with you in every place,
That you may have victory over your enemies.
May God grant you his grace.
Amen.

The Presentation

The Purification[54]

Simeon: I have been a priest in Jerusalem here
And taught God's law many a year,
Hoping in all my mind,
That the time were near at hand
That God's Son should appear
On earth to save mankind.
And that before I died, I might see
My Savior with mine eye,
But it is so long overdue,
That it greatly saddens me.

For I grow old and lose my strength,
And my sight begins to fail.
I would feel even greater sorrow, except that
As I will truly tell you:
God in his grace has called on me
To await this blissful birth.
To the Holy of Holies, I will go
To pray God to be my guide,
To comfort me in my sorrow.

Here Simeon kneels and says:

Good God in Trinity,
How long must I wait
Till you will send your Son
That I might see Him here on earth?
Good Lord, have pity on me!

My life is quickly drawing to an end.
Little strength is left to me.
God Lord, send down your Son,
That I might worship Him,
If I can, while I still have all my faculties.*   *mind

Both with my feet and my two hands
I go to hold Him,
And certainly [I wish] to see Him with my eyes,

---

54 Candlemass, Feb.2nd, has historically been celebrated throughout the Christian world, though less commonly in advanced countries in the past century. The celebration derives from Mosaic Law, where a woman presented herself forty days after giving birth for purification, offering sacrifice, and at that time presenting her child to the Temple. There are a number of variants of this play in England, which would attest to its popularity and the widespread knowledge of the event. (Some plays conflate Candlemass and Jesus' meeting with the doctors in the Temple twelve years later.)

To speak to Him with my tongue,
And to work all my limbs
Readily in service to Him.
My sovereign Lord, send forth your Son,
Quickly, without tarrying,
For I would be glad to leave this world!
It is burdensome to me.

Angel: Simeon, cease your piteous complaint,
Your prayer is heard in heaven.
Make your way quickly to Jerusalem,
And assuredly there you will see
He that is the Son of God that you speak of.
In the temple there that you dwell in—
He shall make light and purify
The darkness of Original Sin.
And now the deed will begin
That has been prophesized and spoken of.   50

Simeon: I thank thee, Lord of Grace,
That has granted me the time and space
To live and await this.
I will now walk to the place
Where I may see thy Son's face,
Which will be my joy and bliss!
Indeed, I never felt lighter,
When I had to walk there before!
For it is a merry time now,
That my Lord, God, is born.

Prophetess Anna: Hail, Simeon, what news do you have?
What makes you so full of joy?
Tell me where you are going.

Simeon: Anne, prophetess, if you knew why
I promise, you would go too,
And all men [that are] living.
For as I proclaim, God's Son
Is born to redeem mankind!
Our Savior is come to put an end to our sorrow!
Therefore, I go forth in great joy.
And that is the reason I hurry
To our temple, to see Him,
So don't detain me, good friend.

Anna: Now blessed is God in Trinity!
Since that time has come to pass!
And I will go with you
To finally see my Savior,
And also worship Him
With all my will and all my mind,
I will now do this as I am bound to do.

And then both of them go to the temple.

Simeon: Truth be told, in the temple of God,
This day shall be solemnly offered
He who is the king of all,
He that shall be scourged and shed his blood,
And after, die on the cross,
For no just cause;
For whose Passion shall befall,
Such a sorrow both sharp and painful,
That it shall be as a sword that pierces
Through his mother's heart.

Anna, prophetess: Yes, it shall be as I have said,
For the redemption of all mankind,
To restore the bliss
That had been lost to us all [until this time],
By our father of our own kind
Adam and Eve who came before us.

Mary: Joseph, my husband,
Indeed, you know that it is nearly forty days,
Since my son's birth.
Therefore, certainly, we must go to the temple   100
To offer our Son of Bliss
Up to his Father on high.
And I in God's sight
Must be purified,
My soul cleansed with all my might
In the presence of the Trinity.

Joseph: You have no need to be purified
Nor to offer your Son, God help me:
First, you are pure,
Undefiled in thought and deed.
And another reason, without a doubt is that your Son,
Is to mediate between God and man.
Therefore it is unnecessary,

Yet to uphold the law of Moses
The two of us shall take between us
Doves and turtledoves to sacrifice.

They go to the temple.

Simeon: All hail, my kindly comforter!

Anna Prophetess: All hail, mankind's creator!

Simeon: All hail, you God of Might!

Anna Prophetess: All hail, mankind's Savior!

Simeon: All hail, both king and emperor!

Anna Prophetess: All hail, as it is right!

Simeon: All hail, also Mary bright!

Anna Prophetess: All hail, healer of illness!

Simeon: All hail, lantern of light.

Anna Prophetess: All hail, you mother of meekness!

Mary: Simeon, I understand and see
That you have knowledge that
Both my Son and I are clean.
Also, my Son deserves to be
In your company,
And, therefore I have brought Him here.

Simeon welcomes Jesus.

Simeon: Welcome, prince without peer!
Welcome, God's own Son!
Welcome, my Lord so dear!
Welcome, come dwell with me.

We receive your mercy, O God.[55]

Lord God, in majesty:
We have received this day from Thee,

---

55   Psalm 47:10 is spoken by those present at this point.

Thy great mercy, as we may see here
In the midst of thy temple.
Therefore, let thy reverent name
Be worshipped in every manner,
Over all this world, both far and near,
Even to the uttermost end;
For now, man is delivered from danger,
And rest and peace will come to all mankind.

"Now you dismiss your servant" etc.[56] *While the verses of the psalm are sung, Simeon plays with the child, and when it ends, he says,*

Lord, now let me die and pass away,
For I, thy servant in this place,
Have seen my dear Savior,
Which Thou hath ordained to openly appear   150
Before the face of all mankind
At this determined time:
Thy light shines clear;
He is the salvation for all mankind.
Mary, now take your child here
And guard Him well; He who is man's salvation.

Anna Prophetess: Now, I am not reluctant to die either,
For more than four score and two years,*   *eighty-two
I have waited to see this event,
And since that it has come,
Whatever God's will is for me,
Right so must it be.

Joseph: Take these three candles—
Mary, Simeon, and Anne—
And I shall take the fourth for myself
And then offer our child up.

Mary: Highest Father, God of power:
I offer your own dear Son to You here,
As I am sworn to do by your law.
Receive this child gladly,
For he is the first, this child so dear,
That is born of his mother.
Yet, though I offer Him to You,
Good Lord, yet give Him to me again,

---

56   This is called the "Canticle of Simeon" and is sung at compline.

For my comfort would be lost,
If we were apart for long.

Mary lays the child on the altar.

Joseph: Now sir priest of the temple,
I have five pence to give you,
And our child we take again.
It is the law, as you well know.

Priest: Joseph, you have done the right thing,
For your child's sake.
Yet another offering you must make,
And therefore take your Son, Mary,
Much joy you may experience during your waking hours,
While He is in your company.

Mary: Therefore, I am very glad and happy
To receive my child again,
Else I would be blameworthy;
And certainly afterwards, I am willing   200
To offer to God,
Both wild and tame fowl.
In my Son's name,
I shall never grow weary of doing God's service.

Joseph: Here Mary are the same [ones that we brought to offer in sacrifice]
To do the duties of Holy Church.

Mary offers the fowls on the altar and says,

Mary: Almighty Father, merciful King:
Receive now this little offering,
For it is the best that can be offered
By your little child so young
Presented by me to You today,
To your high majesty.
[From out] of his simple poverty
By his devotion and my good will,
As is fitting, unto your altar receive
Your Son's offering from me.

The Appearance to Mary[57]

(excerpt from The Harrowing of Hell 2, Appearance
to Mary; Pilate and the Soldiers ll. 73-136)

Then the soul of Jesus goes to revive his body, and having done so, he says,

Jesus: I have travelled difficult paths
And suffered many great pains,
Stumbled at the stake and at the stone
For nearly thirty-three years.
I alit from my Father's throne
To redress man's sorrow.
My flesh was beaten to the bone;
I bled my pure blood.

For man's love, I suffered death.
And for man's love, I have quickly risen;
I have made my body bread for man,
To feed his soul.
Man, you have let me go,
And will not follow after me now.
You will never find another such friend
To help you in your time of need.

Hail, holy mother, my mother dear![58]
All hail, mother, with glad cheer!
For now, my pure body has arisen,
Your Son that was buried deep,
On this third day, as I foretold to you,
[How that] I should rise out of the cold clay.
Now I have come forth boldly,
Therefore, do not weep anymore.

Mary: Welcome my Lord, welcome my grace!
Welcome my Son and my solace!
I shall worship Thee in every place.
Welcome, Lord God of Might!   100
I suffered great sorrow in my heart
When You were laid in death's bed,

---

57   Immediately after the "Harrowing of Hell 2," and before the next play where Christ appears to Mary
      Magdalene, and Peter and John at the tomb, *N-Town* contains a brief passage where Christ visits his
      mother. Anecdotal stories demonstrating popular belief in such an event can also be found in *The
      Book of Margery Kempe*, where Margery speaks of a vision of such a visit to the Virgin.
58   Echoes Gabriel's salutation.

But now my bliss is newly born;
All men will rejoice in this sight.

Jesus: All this world that was lost
Shall worship you, both morning and evening;
For had I not been born of you,
Man would have been lost, to remained forever in hell.
I was dead, and now I live;
And through my death, I have saved man,
For now, I have risen out of my grave,
And in heaven, man shall now dwell.

Mary: Dear Son, these are good words,
You have comforted me in my mourning.
Blessed be thy precious blood
That has saved mankind.

Jesus: Now, dear mother, I take my leave of you.
Be of joyful heart and mood,
For death is dead, and life does wake,
Now that I am risen from my grave.

Mary: Farwell, my Son! Farwell, my child!
Farwell My Lord, My God so mild!
My heart is healed that at first despaired.
Farwell, my own dear love!
Now, all mankind be joyful,
For death is dead, as you may now see!
And life is raised, to endlessly
Dwell above in heaven.

When my Son was nailed on the tree,
All women mourned with me,
For certainly greater sorrow could not be known
Than I suffered.
But this joy now passes all sorrow,
For all that my child suffered on that harsh morning,
Now He is the redeemer of us all
And brings us all to bliss.

Death and Assumption of the Virgin

The Assumption of Mary

May God the Father and His Mother be present to assist my work.

Doctor:[59] Right worshipful lords, if you like you will hear,
Of the Assumption of the glorious Mother Mary
That Saint John the Evangelist wrote and taught,
In the book called the Apocrypha, as I have read without a doubt.[60]
At the age of fourteen she conceived Christ in her pure state,
And in her fifteenth year, she gave birth, as I dare to declare,

---

59 Another expositor like Contemplation.
60 The assumption of Mary is based on apocryphal texts dating back to the fourth and fifth century.
Though her corporeal assumption was debated throughout history and texts are not definitive on
this issue, the Catholic Church dogmatically endorsed the event from the late fifteenth century on.
The play is based on the "First and Second Latin Form of the Passing of Mary" and the apocryphal
"Account of the Falling Asleep of the Holy Mother of God" attributed to John. This play is believed
to be a late addition to the Mary material, and shows signs of being written by a different author than
those of the previous Marion materials.

Here on earth, living with that sweet Son thirty-three years,
And after his death, she endured twelve years.
Now deftly calculate those years [with] me:
And I see the age of this maid Mary,
When she ascended above the archangels,
[Was] three score* year, as Scripture does specify,   *sixty
[As] the author of *The Saint's Legend* truly attests.[61]

She dwelt in Israel by Mount Sion
After the Ascension of her son, incarnated.[62]
All the holy places on earth that Christ dwelt in,[63]
Devoutly she visited, honoring the Godhead.
First, the place where Christ was baptized called the river Jordan,
Then to where He fasted and was [arrested under] malicious, false charges,
To where He was buried and victoriously rose alone,
To where He ascended to heaven, God in his humanity.
As I read, this is how she occupied herself,
And she prayed a great deal in the temple.
Now we proclaim, she is blessed.

And men will perform her ascension here [upon the stage],
Praying that you, the audience, watch and pay attention.

Soldier: Peace, stop blabbering in the devil's name!
So that you will not seem to be horrid bitches!
Our worthy princes are gathered together,
Men of high station, that are lords of this land.
By their high wisdom, they shall now decide
How all Israel must be governed.
And the tonsured priests[64] that have besmirched our laws,
They shall be slain or exiled, as the princes order.
Henceforth, you will dwell in peace
And listen to them. I must be quiet.
Whatever boy cries out, I will kill
Like a knave; I'll kill him with this jagged club!
Now listen to our princes. All kneel!

---

61   The is Jacobus de Voragine's *Golden Legend,* ca. 1260, translated into English by William Caxton
     1275. It is also one of the influential sources for later Mary Magdalene legends.
62   This particular playwright actually presents Mary and Jesus as married in lines 15, 104, 306 rather
     than using the Father, by evoking the unity of the Trinity so that Father and Son are interchangeable.
     I have changed lines 15 and 104 to "incarnation" rather than "born in marriage" for clarity. The
     audience is also invited to think of the image of Christ as bridegroom and virgin nuns as brides, for
     which Mary sets the precedent.
63   In a sense, this becomes the first pilgrimage, setting precedence for all that follow.
64   This connects the disciples of Christ in Biblical times with contemporary monks.

Bishop of Law: Now, you princes, I am a high priest of the law[65]
I ask for an immediate response to this sedition here,
As far as you know, is there any renegade among us
Or any that would use clever eloquence to pervert the people?
If there be, we must all set upon them,
For if they blasphemy our faith, I will prove they are our enemies.
They shall be bound until flies lay eggs in them
And hanged by the gums until the devil makes them groan.
We cannot delay
In dealing with such rascals harshly
That dispute our laws and our scripture.   50
Now let the noble princes in purple
Speak up and save our laws!

Prince 1: Sir, since we slew Him that called himself our king
And said He was God's Son, lord over all,
Since his death I have heard of no such uprising.
And if He had lived, He would have made us all his slaves.

Bishop: Therefore, we were wise to hasten his end;
Who climbs too high, he has a hard fall.

Prince 2: Yet of one thing I will warn you at the start—
His mother, that men call Mary, is living.
Many people attend her.
If we allow her to live,
There is danger that we will be rebuked,
As she will subvert our laws.
And she shall cause us much shame!

Bishop: Ah sir, be bold. Are you afraid of a woman?
What do you think she could do against us?

Princes 3: Sir, there are others in the country that preach
And insist that He is living that we slew!
And if we suffer them to continue, they will breed a stench,
For through their fair speech they besmirch our laws!
Therefore, upon this bench,*   *judicial/ecclesiastic
We must determine what is best to do to deter them.
We are lost, if they gain hold.

Bishop: Well then, tell me what you intend.

---

65   Here a Jewish high priest. The contemporary audience would see him as Bishop of Law of the
ecclesiastic court.

Prince 1: Let us imprison them until their power is destroyed!

Prince 2: Better to beat them to death!

Prince 3: Nay, best to torture and hang them!

Bishop: No, sirs, not so. You best consider
What you plan now and what may happen after:
If we slay them, it will cause the common people to rise up.[66]
Better the devil slay them, then we should let that happen.
But once that sister is dead—Mary that old wench—
We shall burn her body and hide the ashes,
And disgrace her as best we can,
And then slay those disciples that travel from afar to attend her
And cut their bodies into pieces!
Do you not think this is the best plan?

Prince 1: We are very pleased with your wise counsel.

Bishop: Then, knights, I charge you to be prepared!
You, tormentors, make ready!
When Mary is dead,
And the sooner the better, the devil smite off her head!

Mary is in the temple, praying and saying,

Mary: O high Wisdom,[67] in your noble deity,
Your infinite humility made our salvation possible
When it pleased You, by taking on humanity most simply through me.
With the obedience I owe You, I offer You thanks.
And glorious Lord and Son, if it pleases your benignity,
Not to displease You with my desire—
I long to be your presence, joined to the Unity.*   *trinity 100

All my heart and soul naturally desires
To be with You in your domination,
As all creatures who have faith in You.
And much more I owe You, your mother by your incarnation,
Desiring your presence, who was given our form,
When You were born God and man of my body.

Wisdom (Jesus): My sweet mother's prayer ascends to Me.
Her holy heart and her love is all for Me,

---

66   He rightly fears making martyrs of them.
67   Wisdom is one of the names (qualities) of Christ.

Therefore, angel, you shall now descend to her.
Tell her she shall come to my eternity.
I extend my abundant mercy to her,
Receiving her into joy, from worldly perplexity,
And as a token of this, this palm I now proffer her,
Say to her, she need not fear any adversity.

Angel 1: By your might, I descend to your mother in virginity,

Angel 2: Delivering your message of heavenly fellowship.

An angel descends, with citharas playing, and says to Mary,

Angel 1: Hail, excellent princess, Mary most pure!
Hail, radiant star, the sun is not as bright!
Hail, Mother of Mercy and most demure maid!
The blessing that God gave Jacob now alights upon you!

Mary: Now welcome, bright bird, God's angel, I believe!
You are the messenger of the Almighty; I welcome you with all my strength.
I beseech you, tell me now, as you are most courteous,
What is the name given to you?

Angel 1: Why do you desire to know my name, lady?

Mary: Gracious angel, I beseech you since you are the messenger.

Angel 1: My name is great and marvelous. Truth to tell,
The high God, your Son will dwell with you in bliss.
On the third day from now, you will expire
And ascend into the presence of your Son, my God.

Mary: Mercy, great mercy, God, now I say,
Indeed, thank you, sweet angel for this message.

Angel 1: In token, lady, I am presenting to you
A branch, of a palm that comes from paradise.
God bids that is be bore before your bier.

Mary: Now, thanks be to the Lord in his eternal mercy!

Angel 1: Your meekness, your humility, and your great learning
Is most pleasing in the sight of the Trinity.
Your royal seat in heaven is prepared.
Now ready yourself to die, your Son will then raise you.

Mary: I obey the commandment of my God,
The Lord of Might, but before that, one thing I ask:
That my brethren, the apostles, might come before me
And see me, before I pass into that light.
But they are so scattered, I believe it cannot be.

Angel 1: Lady, truly you know, nothing is impossible for God.
For He that sent Habakkuk with food to Babylon from Jewry,
To Daniel in the den of lions, the prophet
By a hair on his head, is so mighty!
By the same might, God may bring the apostles here to attend you!   150
Therefore do not let your mind be disturbed, lady.

Mary: I am no more, glorious divine angel.
And I beseech my Son that I do not see the fiend,
Until the time I pass out of this world.
His horrible look would greatly frighten me;
There is nothing I fear but his awful presence.

Angel 1: Gracious empress, what do you have to fear?
Since the fruit of your body overcame Lucifer's violence.
That horrible serpent dare not approach you,
And your blossom [Jesus,] shall oppose him
Should he attempt it.
Do you desire anything beside this right now?

Mary: Nothing but to be blessed by God's might.

Angel 1: I recommend myself to you, most excellent in my sight,
And with this [said] I ascend again to God.

   The angel ascends.

Mary: Now Lord, with my humility, I bless your sweet name
Which heaven and earth endlessly celebrate in song.
If it pleases You in your mercy, guide my simple soul
To magnify your name.
Now holy maidens, servants of God, I believe
I shall pass from this world as the angel confirms.
Therefore, I tell you now I propose to go
To my simple dwelling, beseeching your reply
That you will assiduously watch me both day and night.

Virgin 1: We shall, gracious lady, with all our might.
You shall pass from us, that is our sweet sun of succor,

That is our singular solace, radiant is your light,
Your painful absence shall bring me great despair.

Virgin 2: Most excellent princess fixed in all virtue:
In all heaven and earth, lady, you are honored.
We shall watch over you as is right and due to you
Until the time that you pass to that high tower [of heaven]
With . . .

Mary: God thanks you and so do I.
Now I will make myself ready for this journey.
I wish to God my brethren were here with me,
To bear my body [as before they] bore Jesus our Savior.

St. John the apostle suddenly appears before Mary's door.

John: Wonderful God, great is thy might,
You have worked many wonders, as You have willed.
I was preaching in Ephesus, a far away country,
And by a white cloud, I was brought to these hills.
I see Christ's mother dwelling here.
Some marvelous messages is coming to that maiden.
I will go and salute that bird who is most bright in virtue
And find out the reason for my sudden[ly] coming [to her].

Here he will knock on the door, enter Mary's house and say to her:

Hail, Mother Mary, perpetual maiden!

Mary: Welcome with all my glad heart, virgin John!
Joyful of your presence, my heart begins to swoon.
Think you not, John, on how my eternal child,
Said these words to us when He hanged upon the cross?   200
"Here is your son, woman," so He bade me call you,
And you to call me, "Mother," each to gratify the other.
He there entrusted the keeping of my earthy body to you,
One maid to another, as seemed proper.
And now that gracious Lord has sent you to me, my son.

John: Now, good fair lady, what is there to do?
Tell me why I have been called here.

Mary: Sweet son John, so I will.
Our Lord God recently sent a gleaming angel to me
Who said [that] I should pass to where three are as one;
Then I asked the angel that you be present.

John: Oh holy mother, shall you go from us?
My brethren will be aggrieved by this news and will mourn
That you shall go from us!
You continue to send us much tribulation, Lord.
You, our master and comfort ascended from us,
And now our joy, your mother, you intend to take.
Then all our comfort will be gone from us.
What did the angel say to you mother, anything more?

Mary: He brought me this palm from my Son there,
Which I beseech, as the angel bade me,
That you bear before my bier,
Devoutly and solemnly saying my dirge.
For John, I have heard that the Jews talk about me a good deal.

John: Good lady, what have you heard?

Mary: Secretly, in their council they have ordered
When my soul has passed into God's bliss
That my body be burned and shamefully destroyed,
Since Jesus was born of me, and they slew Him with their hands!
And therefore, I beseech you, John, both flesh and skin,
Help to ensure that I am buried, for I put my trust in you.

John: Fear not lady, for I shall stay with you.
By God, I wish my brethren were here now and knew this.

Suddenly all the apostles appear before the door, marveling.

Peter: Holy brethren! In grace we meet here now!
Lord God, what is the reason for this sudden gathering?
Now, sweet brother Paul, will you take it upon yourself
To pray to God for all of us that we may understand his will.

Paul: Now, good brother Peter, how should I pray here
That am the least worthy of this congregation?
I am not worthy to be called an apostle, truly I say to you,
For like a madman I abused Holy Church[68]
But nevertheless, I am by the grace of God humbled by that.

Peter: Great is your humility evermore brother, Paul.

Paul: Peter, God has entrusted you with the keys of heaven,
And you are the pillar of light and prince of us all!

---

68   The reference is to Acts 9:1-5, Paul's conversion.

It is most fitting that you make this prayer,
And I, though unworthy, will pray here with you.

Peter: I will undertake this, for your sake, Paul.
Now almighty God that sits in the angelic hall above,
With our hands we make the sign of thy Holy Cross,   250
Beseeching You to send your mercy down on us.
And if it pleases You, tell us why we are brought together here.

John: Holy brethren, you are welcome [here].
I shall tell you why we are all brought together here:
For Mary, God's mother, was sent a message
That she shall go from this wretched world to bliss,
And desired to have us present at her dying.

Peter: Brother John, we may sigh and mourn
At these tidings, and that will not displease God.

Paul: Truly, we may grieve evermore, Peter,
That our mother and our comfort should be absent from us.
But nonetheless, the will of God must be fulfilled.

John: That is well said, Paul but henceforth beware.
That none of you make her death known by your mourning,
For then it should be immediately known by the Jews
Who would say that we fear death, and that is against what we teach.
For we say all those who believe in the Holy Trinity,
Shall live forever and not die; this truly we preach.
And if we grieve for her, then it will be said:
"Those preachers, they, themselves, fear death too much."
And therefore, in God, now let everyone be glad!

Peter: We shall do as you tell us, holy brother John.
Now we beseech you, let us see our dear mother, Mary.

John: Now in God's name, then, let us go to her.
She will be very glad to see this holy company.
Peter: Hail, mother and maiden! Never was there anyone
So blessed as you, truly!

Paul: Hail, incomparable queen, God's holy throne!
Of you sprang salvation and all our glory!
Hail, mankind's mediator and mender of sin!

Mary: With all my holy heart, brother, you are certainly welcome!
I beseech you now to tell me about your sudden appearance.

Peter: In diverse countries we preached of your Son and his bliss.
Suddenly, various clouds covered each of us.
And we were brought before your gate here, indeed.
No man could tell us why we were brought here.

Mary: Now I thank God for his mercy! This is a great miracle!
Now I shall tell you why my Son has brought these things to pass.
I desired to be in his presence.

John: No wonder, lady, that you did so.

Mary: Then my son, Jesus, in his pity,
Sent an angel to me, and then He said,
That on the third night I should ascend to my Son in the Deity.
Then I heartily prayed to have you present, brethren,
And thus at my request, God has sent you to me.

Peter: Wise, gracious lady, we are pleased to do so.

Mary: Blessed brethren, I then beseech you to attend me.
Now I will rest in this bed that has been prepared for me.
Watch me diligently with your lamps and lights.

Paul: We shall prepare all things for your death, lady.   300

Mary: Now you shall soon see God's might.
My earthly flesh grows faint.

Here she shall be appropriately adorned in a bed.

Peter: Brethren, right now each of you take a candle,
And hastily light them as our mother still lives,
And let us intently watch in the virgin's presence,
So that when the Lord comes to his virgin bride,
He may find us awake and ready with our lights,[69]
For we do not know for certain the hour of his coming.
And in purity, see that you all are ready!

Mary: Sweet Son, Jesus, now I beseech your mercy!
Let thy mercy spread over all the sinful people![70]

Here the Lord descends with all of the heavenly court and says,

---

69   Invokes comparison to Gethsemane, but now the apostles do stay awake and attend.
70   Mary as intermediate, interceding for man, see also line 280.

God: The voice of my mother draws me closer.
I descend to her of whom I was born.

Here organs play.

Mary: Welcome, gracious Lord! Jesus, Son and God of Mercy!
An angel would have sufficed me in my need, High King.

God: Mother, in my own person, I will be ready
With this heavenly choir to orchestrate your dirge:
Come, my chosen one, and I will set you on my throne, [71]
Because the King desires your beauty.

Mary: My heart is ready Lord, my heart is ready,
I will sing and recite a psalm for the Lord.

Apostles: This is she that knew no iniquity abed.
She shall rest among holy souls.

Mary: All generations will call me blessed,
For He who is mighty has done great things for me, and holy is his name.

God: I came from Lebanon my bride, come that you be crowned.

Mary: Behold I come, as it is written in the book regarding me,
So that I may do your will, my God;
My spirit rejoices in God my Savior.

Here Mary's spirit departs from her body into God's bosom.[72]

God: Now come my sweet cleanest and most pure soul
And rest in my most bright bosom.
All my apostles, take care of this body.
In the Valley of Jehoshaphat, there you shall find
A newly made grave for Mary's sepulcher.
Bear this body solemnly
And assuredly await me there for three days,
And I shall appear to you again and comfort you in your adversity.
With this sweet soul, I now ascend away from you.

---

71 Lines 318-329 are written in Latin and in couplets, elevating and celebrating the passing of Mary. God is Jesus in the play; the audience is invited to continually consider the Trinity in which Father and Son are united.

72 In both the "Second Latin Form" and "The Account by St. John," Mary's soul is received into heaven and then returns to earth to claim her body that then, too, ascends to heaven. (In the "First Latin Form," the soul still ascends first, and later the body is seen ascending by St. Thomas.) Here, we also have a prefiguring of the Last Judgment.

Peter: In our tribulations, Lord, protect us.
We have no comfort on earth but You.
Sweet soul of Mary, pray that your Son defends us.
Remember your poor brethren when they come to your throne.

Chorus of Martyrs: Who is this who ascends from the wilderness,
Flowing with delights, leaning on her beloved?

Order of Angels: She is the most beautiful of the daughters of Jerusalem,
  as you have seen.[73]
Full of charity and love, and so assumed into heaven in joy
To be seated on her throne of glory at the right hand of the Son.

   All the heavenly court sings.

First Virgin: Now sister, I beseech you, let us attend you.
And wash your glorious body that is here in our sight,
As is the custom* observed by us.   *religious law 350
Now, blessed be this person that bore the God of Might.

Second Virgin: Sister, I am ready with all my faith,
To wash and worship this very bright body,
All creatures owe you due obeisance,
For this body received the spirit of the Holy Ghost.

   And they kiss Mary's body.

John: Now, holy brother Peter, I heartily pray you
To bear this holy palm before this glorious body,
For you are prince of apostles and head of our company.
Therefore, it seems this office truly befalls you.

Peter: Certainly, and you who slept on Christ's breast, seeing heaven—[74]
You are God's clean maid, without a doubt.
It is most befitting that you do this office
Therefore take it upon yourself, brother, we pray you.
And I shall help bear the bier.

Paul: And I, Peter, with all our brothers,
Will help lay this blissful body in the ground.
We take this holy corpse up now,
Devoutly speaking our observance.

---

73   Lines 343-47 are in Latin, elevating and celebrating the Assumption of the Virgin. They are couplets
     from Jacobus de Voragine's *Golden Legend.*

74   Peter is referring to the fact that Revelations is attribute to John, as well as calling upon him, since
     the apocryphal "Account of the Falling Asleep of the Holy Mother of God" is also attributed to him.

Here they will bear the body, carrying their lights too.

Peter: Israel went from Egypt and the house of Jacob departed from barbarous
people. Alleluia.[75]

Apostle: Judea became his sanctuary, Israel his realm. Alleluia.

The angels sweetly sing in heaven, "alleluia."

Bishop: Hark, sir princes! What noise is this?
The earth and the air are filled with song!
I never heard such a sound, certainly!
Can you tell what it signifies?

Prince 1: By my God of much might, I do not know
Whosoever they be, loudly they sing!
I am afraid there will be something amiss.
It would be good if we secretly spied
[To discover] what is happening out there.

Princes 2: I have now lived threescore* years,   *sixty
But I have never heard such a sound before!
My heart begins to shutter and quake for fear!
I do not doubt that there is some new sorrow that has sprung up.

Princes 3: Yes, truly, that there is, I say to you.
The prophet's mother, Mary, is dead.
The disciples bear her in ceremony,
Celebrating despite our authority.

Bishop: Fie on those lousy dogs! They need to be stopped.
Out, the devil is in my head!
You dumbfounded princes, do something quickly,
Or I swear to Mohammad—your bodies shall bleed![76]
Now, that queen is dead.
You cowardly knights in armor
And you tormentors, our time is up.
Quickly, rascals, go out the gates.
And bring me that vile body, I order you!

Prince 1: Have no doubt, sir bishop, lest we disgrace ourselves,
We shall do shame to that body and those preachers.

---

75   Line 369-370 are in Latin.
76   While in the earliest sources, the disbelievers are Jews, in this play, Judaism and Islam are conflated
      and presented as enemies of the Christianity. This anti-Islamic sentiment, from the Crusades, is also
      found in the *Digby Magdalene.*

Prince 2: Sir, I shall get those blabbers or greatly harm them!   400
Those tainted traitors shall suffer, if I gaze down upon them.

Prince 3: I would gladly attack those rascals.
I shall entrap those snivelers with very sharp blows.

Bishop: Go hence, in the devil's name, and get me that churl!
And bring that vile body to me before these towers!
And slay those disciples!
Go forth scoundrels, at once!
The devil's boys may break your bones![77]
Go stop that body with your stones!
Out! Go! I am going crazy!

> *The princes and their ministers descend like ferocious animals and dash their heads against rocks.*

Prince 2: Devil! Where is this company?*   *Mary's entourage
I hear the noise, but I see nothing.
Alas, I have lost all my strength!
I am full of woe! I have gone crazy!

Prince 3: I am so afraid; I would gladly flee!
Let the devil carry him off who brought me here!
I run; I run around. Woe is me!
Madness has overcome me!
I don't care if I die.

Prince 1: Cowards! Fie upon you!
Are you afraid of a dead body?
I shall go there boldly!
I don't fear that company at all!

> *This crazy prince leaps into Mary's bier and hangs by his hands.*

Alas, my body is full of pain!
I am glued to this bier!
My hands are withered, both of them[78]

---

77   The princes and their entourage are threatened with torture if they fail in their mission.
78   As in "The Nativity," the disbeliever's hands wither, and Mary is the instrument for bringing right belief and conversion. Both the Virgin Mary and Mary Magdalene, in later medieval tradition, are thus presented as having the power to lead disbelievers to the true faith, like the male apostles. However, they do not perform sacraments such as baptism. Here the Virgin is the source of the miracle that is the instrument of conversion; Peter blesses the new convert (symbolically baptism) and sends him forth on a mission off to convert others (an apostolic mission).

Oh, Peter, now pray to thy God for me, here!
When you were brought to Caiphas' court
And a maid accused you there—
I helped you. Now help me in return!
Make me whole from this woeful condition!
Teach me some medicine!

Peter: Sir, I may not aid you in this hour,
For I must attend to this honorable body,
But nevertheless, believe in Jesus Christ, our Savior,
And this that was his mother that we bear on bier.

Prince 1: I believe in Jesus, man's salvation!

Peter: In God's name, then kneel and honor this body.

Prince 1: Now have mercy God and grant me salvation.
I promise to believe in Jesus and his mother.

Peter: Then take this holy palm and go to your nation.
And bid them believe in God; if they will be pure,
Touch them with it on head and hand and face,
And of their illnesses, they shall be cured
And all their other pains ended.

Prince 1: Thank you, holy father Peter!
I shall do as you have taught me here,
With great repentance and humble heart.

Here they carry the bier to the sepulcher.

Peter: Now, holy brethren, let us take this body,
And we will lay it in the grave with great worship,   450
All at once kissing it, for her Son's sake.
Now, burn incense, and we shall put her in this cave.

Here they put the body in the tomb, incense it, and sing.

John: Out of earth You formed me, and in flesh You clothed me,
O Lord, My Redeemer, raise me up on the last day.
Now God, bless this body, as we make the sign of the cross.
Here, as one, we will bless the body in the name of the Father, Son, and Holy
Spirit.

The fruit that is bore, shall save our souls.
Now let us rest, brethren, upon this open grave

Until we have tidings from our Lord and our God,
Here, we wait steadfast in our belief.

Paul: We must do as you say John,
Wait here and pray,
Beseeching Him of comfort that best may provide it,
As we wait about this grave.

Here the prince bearing a palm goes to the Jews.

Prince 1: You Jews that languish in great infirmity,
Believe in Jesus Christ, and you shall have health!
Through virtue of this holy palm that comes from the Trinity
Your sickness shall be assuaged and you shall be restored to health.

Prince 2: I believe in Jesus Christ, God's Son in unity
And forsake my idols, false in their filth.[79]

Here he touches the believers with the palm, and they are healed.

Thank you gracious Lord, and the mother of pity.

Prince 3: What, rascals? Have you forsaken our laws?

Prince 2: I thought it was best thing to do.

Prince 3: In the devil's name then go hence from me!
I die, alas!
The wild devils are tearing me apart!

Demon 1: Hark, Beelzebub and Belial, Sir Satan in the pit:
Let us fetch our servants to this prison!
Blow flames of fire to make them burn!
Demon, make that place ready for when we return again with them!

Demon 2: Quickly let us run and get those rascals
To cast them down deep into this pit here!
They shall burn and boil and freeze in our den![80]

---

79   Note that at this point the Jews are called idol worshippers and aligned with pagans. This does not
     occur in the earlier Mary plays, where the Jewish religion is treated more reverently, and their authors
     treat Judaism as a precursor to Christianity and Christianity as a fulfillment of Jewish prophecy. This
     further suggests that this play was written by a different author than earlier *N-Town* plays (and that
     all the plays were not written by one person). The movement from treating Judaism reverently to
     anti-Semitism is also found in the *Digby Mary Magdalene*. It is also interesting to note, given that the
     Assumption materials are attributed to John, that John's gospel was, in part, directing Jews to convert
     to Christianity.
80   As in Dante's *Inferno,* hell is not just a pit of fire; it includes extreme cold as well.

In the devil's name, now we go as fast as we can!
Whoa! We come into the town.

Demon 1: We will quickly drag these scoundrels
To lie in the pit of hell!

Demon 2: Hell's hounds, go now and bay,
So Sir Satan can hear your cry!

God: Now, angel and all the celestial court,
To earth now descend with Me
To raise the body of my terrestrial mother
And we will bring it to the bliss of my deity.
Do you all assent in unity?

Angel: Yes, for your high mercy Lord, as heaven makes music!

He descends to the apostles and says,

God: Peace be with you all, my apostles dear!
Now I am here before you, your Lord and your God.

Peter: Welcome Christ, our comfort, in thy pure manhood!
Great marvelous God, your might is great!

God: What worship and grace does it seem fitting to you here   500
That I should do to this body that is called Mary?

John: Lord, as You rose from death and reign in thy realm,
So raise this body into divine bliss,
This seems right to us.

Michael: Yes, glorious God, the soul is ready here now
To be joined to the blessed body, if it pleases You.
Heaven and earth would think this the best,
Inasmuch as she bore You, God in your might.

Here the spirit enters Mary's body.

God: Go again into that body blessed soul!
Arise now, my dove, my neighbor, and my sweet friend!
Tabernacle of joy, vessel of life, heavenly temple to reign.
You shall have the bliss that never ends with me, mother:
For as you were clean of the stain of sin on earth,
So you shall reign in heaven, purest of mind.

Mary: Endless worship be offered to you, Jesus, releaser of pain!
I and all of earth who come of our kind may bless You.[81]
I am ready to go with You.

God: Above into heaven, we will ascend then, mother,
To dwell in eternal bliss.

Michael: Heaven and earth now may rejoice,
For God, through Mary, is made man's friend.[82]

With organs playing, they ascend into heaven.

Mary, you are taken into heaven.

God: It pleases the Holy Trinity to honor you, mother.
Therefore, I crown you here in the kingdom of glory.
Of all my chosen, you shall be called
Queen of Heaven and Mother of Mercy.

Michael: We now proclaim, blessed be your name,
For this holy assumption, all heaven sings,
Glory to God!

---

81   An interesting call to Christians, since before "our kin" were the descendants of the Jewish patriarchs.
82   Here Michael not only affirms Mary's part in the salvation story, he also presents her as an intermediate/intercessor working on man's behalf.

Mary Magdalene

The Digby Mary Magdalene[83]

Rome—The Stage of the Emperor

The emperor enters.

Tiberius, Emperor of Rome: Scribe, I command you, and will punish you if you do
Other than tell the audience here,
That I will have it known to all the world,
That I am the chief ruler of heaven and hell.
No one is equal to me in magnificence,
For I am the greatest sovereign of all sovereigns.
All are incomparable to my empire.
Tiberius Caesar, whose power is most potent,
I am royal blood of the greatest royal stock.
The most noble of all emperors and kings born,
And all realms obey my mighty will.
One's life, limb, and possession are all at my behest.
Of all sovereigns, my magnificence is the mightiest
And cannot be denied by neither friend nor foe.
All must abide my judgment and submit to me, as I desire.
All grace upon earth comes from my goodness,[84]
And that brings all people happiness.
I, the most worthy, will now sit upon my throne.

Scribe: Sir, from your person, all grace flows.

Tiberius: For your answer, Belial* bless you!   *a devil
I begin to gain great wealth;
I am wrapped in prosperity and protected from woe.
Hark provost, I command you, [that under me]
All your people live peacefully!
If any refuse to worship my gods,
Let me know, and detain the insurgents,
And I will command the death
Of those who preach of Christ incarnation.

Provost: Lord of lord, I shall spread your command.

Exits.

---

83   The play is done in the round. At the center is the Castle of Magdalene, other locations, stages, are
set up on the circumference of the circle.

84   The king is God's emissary on earth. He is both born to his position (hereditary) and divinely chosen.

Emperor: See how all the world obeys my domination!
That person has not been born that dare disobey me.
Scribe, I advise you to see that all my laws
Be obeyed in all regions,
Inquire and observe, each day that dawns,
To see if any people waver
And act contrary to my order in any way
Or grumble or groan at worshipping my golden gods.
I will put the rebels to the death!
If any remain, identify them, and I will deal with them.

Scribe: It shall be done lord, without delay.

Emperor: Every lord and lady will bow to my law.
Is it not so? Proclaim as one.

All the people acclaim in unity, "Yes, my lord, yes."

Emperor: So, you tenacious people, I am now pleased.
Set the table with wine and spices for my council.
I have now told you my heart, and I am well pleased.
Let us all sit down and make good cheer.

They all sit down to a banquet.

Bethany—Castle of Magdalene

The scene shifts to the Castle of Magdalene where Cyrus lives with his children Mary, Martha, Lazarus, and members of the household.

Cyrus: Emperor and kings and successful conquerors,
Earls and barons and bold knights,   50
Maidens in my garden, so beautiful to the eye,
I command you to obey me at once.
Behold my person, glistening in gold,
Most glorious of all men!
Cyrus is my name. By the coldest cliffs,[85]
I command you to be obedient to me,
Who will not, I will make them miserable.
I will tie any rebel in knots.
This castle of Magdalene and all the country,
Both, more or less, is under my rule.
Lord of Jerusalem, who dare act against me?
All Bethany is at my bidding.
I am secure in my happiness,

---

85   Probably an oath, implying an extreme, such as "when hell freezes over."

And will be for all posterity,
Since I am a royal and wealthy.
I have a faithful son here,
There is no comelier creature in all God's creation,
And two amiable daughters, fair of face,
Glorious and pleasing to my eye.
Lazarus is my son, who I hold in high regard.
Here is Mary, very fair and feminine,
And Martha, full of beauty and delightful,
Full of womanly virtue and grace.
They console me and fill my heart with joy.
To my knowledge there has been no greater devotion
Demonstrated by any other[to me],
Save alone my lady, their deceased mother.
Now Lazarus, who is their brother,
I give the lordship of Jerusalem to you upon my death,
And Mary [shall have] this castle alone, and nothing else,
And Martha shall have Bethany, I say expressly.
These gifts I give you in truth and proclaim
That I am of sound mind.*   *competent to make decisions

Lazarus: Most reverent father, I thank you heartedly
Of the great kindness you have shown to me!
You have bequeathed me such property,
That I will be provided for all my life.
Now, good Lord, if it be your will,
Grant me grace to live according to your will,
And let us live in peace without discord,
With others who might seek to rule us.

Mary Magdalene: God of peace, our greatest guide,
Your name is sweeter than any honey!
We thank you, father for your royal gifts,
That will keep us forever from poverty.
We will find ourselves secured against hardship,
Comforted against worldly travails.
This abode is fit for the daughter of a king—
This wonderful place, truth to tell.

Martha: O good father of great nobility,   100
To so part with your wealth,
Considering our lowliness,
Protecting us from worldly distress,
On many occasions, you have shown us your magnanimity.
You provide for us very generously.
May you be rewarded by heaven's bliss,

And have the sight of the Lord's face,
When you pass to that place!

Cyrus: Now I rejoice in all my wealth!
I delight in providing for the advancement of my children.
Gentle knights and gentlewomen,
Let us now have wine and spices.

Here they are served wine and spices.

Rome—Return to the stage of the Emperor

Emperor: Provost, scribe, and judges of my realm,
I will send my messenger into the far country,
Into the city of Jerusalem,
To Herod that is regent under me,
And to Pilate, judge of that country,
Informing them of my commands.
Provost, take heed, of my written commands
And tell them,
I command them, that harm will come to them,
If there are any in their country that go against my laws,
Preach against my gods or speak ill of them,
Or that rebel against my laws—
Since [each] is my regent and dwells in that realm
And holds his crown by my will,
If any insurgents remonstrate
Or seditiously grumble against me.

Provost: Sir, they shall be informed of all of this,
So that they may conform to your will and uphold your honor.

Emperor: Now messenger, do not tarry,
And you will have gold as your reward.
Bear these letters to king Herod,
And tell him to make inquires in every country
In his onus as judge over them all.

Messenger: Sovereign, your errand shall be done immediately.
I will hasten as fast as I can
To fulfill your command;
I will not tarry a moment day or night.

The messenger leaves to make his way to Herod.

Jerusalem—The stage shifts to
Herod's castle

Herod, philosophers, soldiers and others.

Herod: Amidst the chaos of this world, be silent immediately!
No noise, lest you anger me.
As I am a true king, by noble Mohammed,
I shall cut off your heads, by Mohammed's bones.
Let the god help you, if I had a sword,
I would cut of your heads and hoods. I command you all:
Bare your heads, you ruffians! Who made you so bold?
I shall make you bow to your royal king!
I will be obeyed throughout the world,
And whosoever will not, who performs wonders.*   *miracles
Against my magnificence, shall be taken into custody   150
And endure hard, cold suffering.
Behold these rich rubies, red as any fire,
With goodly green pearls set around them!
What king is worthy or equal in power to me?
Or in this word, who is more feared
Than is the name of Herod, King of Jerusalem?
Lord of Aleppo, Asia, and Tyre,
Of Hebron, Beersheba, and Bethlehem,
All of these are under my governance.
Lo, all of these I hold without dispute.
No man is equal to me, save only the emperor
Tiberius, whose regent I am.
How say you, philosophers, seeing my rich realm,
Am I not the greatest governor?
Tell me what you think.

Philosopher: Sovereign, if it pleases you, I will say,
Ye are the ruler of the region,
And the most worthy sovereign of all nobility
That ever ruled in Judea,
But, sir, Scripture gives information
And doth say in verses
That a child shall win great renown,
And all the world shall worship him;
"And the nations will walk in your light,
And kings in the brightness of your rising."[86]

Herod: And what say you?

---

86   Isaiah 60:3.

Philosopher 2: The same verses are in my book,
Telling me the same as the Scripture,
Of a mighty duke that shall rise and reign
Who shall reign and rule all Israel.
No king shall prevail against his worthiness.
This is prophesized with great eloquence:
"The scepter will not be withdrawn from Judea
Nor a leader from her loins."[87]

Herod: Out, Out! Now I am most grieved!
You rascals! You dogs! May the devil tear you apart!
I bid you to feast on flaying blows.
A sword, a sword! Slay the louts!
You longbones, scoundrels, take back your prophecy!
The culprit [Jesus] shall be caught, and I will surely flay his followers;
Many shall be murdered for him.

Solider 1: My sovereign, do not be dismayed.
They are fools, lacking eloquence,*   *they don't know what they say
They will be caught and suffer.
They cannot withstand us.

Solider 2: My lord, all shall be brought into your audience.*   *presence
We shall have them under our control.
They shall live according to your rule
Or else be sentenced to death.   200

Herod: This speech pleases me,
And raises my spirits indeed!
Though these ruffians remonstrate against me,
I will not allow any to bear offspring,[88]
That would spread harm in my realm,
Privately or overtly about my land.
While I have such men, I do not need to dread
That He will be subdued, without a doubt.

The emperor's messenger comes in, saying to Herod:

Messenger: Hail, prince bountiful!
Hail, mighty lord most magnificent!
Hail, most deserving to be worshipped
Hail, righteous ruler in thy regency!
My sovereign, Tiberius, chief of chivalry,
Has sent you, his sovereign message

---

87   Genesis 49:10.
88   Reference to Herod's order that all male infants be put to death.

That he desires and prays, specifically, that you
Fulfill his commandment and desire.

Here he takes the letters to the king.

Herod: He can be sure I will not refrain
From accomplishing his commandment;
I will fulfill his intent to win his love,
Whether it required piercing bare flesh with sharp swords
In all countries within this region.
None shall escape our clutches,
For we will fulfill his royal command
And with sword and spear pierce the insurgents through the heart.
Now messenger, take this letter quickly,
And bear it to Pilate so that he may see it.

Messenger: My lord, it shall be done swiftly,
I will make haste.

He starts for Pilate's scaffold.

Jerusalem—The stage of Pilate

Pilate and attendants.

Pilate: Now royally, I reign in the robes of state.
I am known both near and far,
As judge of Jerusalem, truth to say,
Under the emperor, Tiberius Caesar.
Therefore, I advice you all, beware
That you do not violate the law.
For, if you do, I will not spare you.
Your judgment will be that you will be hanged and drawn.
For I am Pilate, Rome's appointed governor,
I will show no pity and will put them to pain,*   *torture them
All those impertinent, renegade robbers.
My good sergeants, what say you?
Regarding what I have said, I will not relent.
Pleasantly sirs, answer me,
So my heart is free from care.

Sergeant 1: As you have said, I consider best,
It will be made know to all among us.

Sergeant 2: To pass judgment on them, I believe is best,
Then shall you be dreaded high and low.

Pilate: Aye! Now my good spirits are restored.

Here comes the emperor's messenger to Pilate.

Messenger: Hail, royal of the realm, who wears the robes of state,
Hail, you, the present peer of princes!   250
Hail, judge of Jerusalem, truth to say!
Tiberius, the emperor, sends this correspondence,
And prays you, as you are his dear friend,
Take heed of this decree
And enforce his laws,
As he hath made you governor.

Here Pilate takes the letter with great reverence.

Pilate: Now, by mighty Mars, I shall set many snares,
To strengthen his laws in any way I can.
I rejoice in his renown and welfare,
And for your tidings, I give you this gold today.

Gives gold.

Messenger: Thank you for your generosity my lord,
For this is a gift of great value.

Pilate: Messenger, to my sovereign you may say,
I commend myself into his service

The messenger leaves.

The stage of the castle Magdalene,
Bethany

Cyrus is dying.

Cyrus: Help, help! I stand in dread!
Sickness has set upon my body.
Help, death will be my reward!
Great God, thou be my guide!
How I am afflicted in both my back and sides.
Now, quickly help me to my bed.
This tears my ribs! I shall never walk forth or ride.
The dint of death is heavier than lead.
Lord, Lord, what shall I do at this time?
Gracious God, have pity on me,

In this world no longer shall I dwell.
I bless you, my children, God be with us!

Cyrus dies suddenly, and then Lazarus says:

Lazarus: Alas, great heaviness descends upon me!
There is no tongue that can tell my sorrow,
So great is the distress that befalls me.
I faint, I falter from this cruel strife,
In this duress I can no longer live,
Unless the God of grace give me some respite.
How my pains attack me!
Lord [help me] withstand this distress!

Mary Magdalene: Omnipotent God, that shall forever reign,
Be his help and soul's succor!
He to whom it is most beneficial to tell our pains,
Since He can relieve our dolor.
He is our mightiest ruler,
Able to relieve us from sorrow.

Martha: I am beset by sad sorrows,
So that I cannot long endure my own life.
These grievous pains nearly drive me mad!
My father's cure is to lie beneath the clover,
He who was once full or merriment and gladness.
May our Lord's mercy be his reward
And may He defend him from great pains of hell.

Lazarus: Now, sisters, our father last will we have read:
This castle is ours, with all the adjacent property [and the wealth associated with
  it].

Martha: Reason dictates that you must be our ruler and governor,   300
And we will dwell with you in an obedient manner.
We will not be separated whatever happens.

Mary: Now, brother and sister, you are welcome,
And therefore I pray specially for you.

*On their respective stages, the King of the World, the Flesh, the Devil
with the Seven Deadly Sins, a Bad Angel, and a Good Angel enter.*

The stage of the World—the World, Pride, and Covetousness

World: I am the World, worthiest realm that God made!
And I am the primary foundation,[89]
Next to heaven, if the truth be known.
See how Scripture acclaims me?
For I am he that shall endure the longest,
Of all dominions.
If I am his foe, who can prosper?
I am the center of the Wheel of Fortune.[90]
In me resides the order of the seven metals,
That which ties together the seven planets.[91]
Gold, pertaining to the sun, astronomers say,
Silver, to the moon, white and pure,
Iron, to Mars, that long may endure,
The fugitive mercury, to Mercury,
Copper, to Venus, shining in his mirror,
The fragile tin, to Jupiter, so it is said,
To the planet Saturn, full of rancor,
Is the soft metal lead, of no great purity.
Lo, all these rich treasures dwell in the World—
The seven princes of hell, earthly wealth.
Now who may presume to rival me in honor?

Pride: Ye worthy World, you are the foundation of happiness,
For all of them that dwell under your dominion.

Covetousness: And whomever refuses you domination,
Will not receive ministrations from me, Covetousness.

World: I pray you don't even make mention of that.
Make them know of my sovereignty,
And then they will gladly be supplicant to me,
If they have any needs.

---

89   World is boasting that, after heaven, he is the source of life.

90   The Wheel of Fortune is a wheel upon which a man is placed. Lady Fortune spins the wheel, and if a man's head stops at the top, he has good fortune, but if it lands at the bottom, his fortune is bad. Fortune is fickle, symbolized by the spinning of the wheel, much like a roulette wheel.

91   The earth was believed to contain seven primary metals in medieval times. Each metal also corresponded to one of the heavenly bodies—recognized as planets.

The Stage of Flesh

Here enters the King of Flesh with Sloth, Gluttony, and Lechery.

Flesh: I, King of Flesh, am adorned with flowers.
I have dominion over delicious dainties,
So royal a king has never been born anywhere,
Who has more delectable delights.
For I have restoratives to comfort me:
Galingale, ambergris, and crushed pearls
Are available to ease all my distress.
And to counteract all noxious things:
Clary, long pepper, and grains of paradise,*   *a spice
Ginger and cinnamon for every occasion.
Lo, all these delicious dainties I use,
With such dainties, I have what gives me pleasure.
Who would desire more mirth and delight
Than to embrace and kiss my fair spouse Lechery?
And by my good judgment, [here] is my knight Gluttony,
Along with the pleasant lady who is seated by my side.
And to say more, here is Sloth another good [companion],   350
A more pleasant company cannot be found anywhere.

Lechery: Oh you, prince, I am full of ardent love,
Glowing with amorousness,
Gladly I would lay with you,
Rewarding your gentility with pleasure.

Flesh: I must kiss you, you beauteous bird!
I lustily desire to hold you immediately.

The Stage of the Devil

Here shall enter the Prince of Devils on the stage, accompanied by Wrath and Envy.
Hell is underneath the stage.

Thus says the Devil:

Satan: Now I, prince well adorned, puffed with pride,
Satan, your sovereign, take advantage of every circumstance,
For in my tower, I am prepared to tempt you at any time.
As a royal king, I am seated as I please,
With Wrath and Envy in my royal retinue.
The boldest [man] in the world I can bend to my will,
Besiege his soul and make it submit to me.

I am angry with men that they should have the joy
That Lucifer and many legions [of angels] lost due to their pride.[92]
The snares that I shall set are greater than those at the fall of Troy;
I will besiege him in every way possible.
I shall rent him from grace, wheresoever he abides;
His body and soul shall enter my stronghold,
I will seize him.
Now my stout knights,
You shall march as a troop with me.
My plan shall provide a scheme for us;
Quickly we will proceed for my sake.

Wrath: In some way, we will win her* with wrath.   *trap Mary Magdalene

Envy: Or with subtleness we will seduce her into sin.
Satan: Off we go then, let us begin
To work some injury upon her.

Here the Devil goes to the World and his company.

The stage of the World

Satan and his followers arrive.

Satan: Hail World, worthiest and most bountiful!
In haste we must have a council,
You and all your companions must apply yourself
To make a woman of good name our servant.

World: Satan, my council and I will assist you.
I pray you to come to my tent.
    Satan and his followers ascend the stage.
I wish that the King of Flesh were here with his retinue.
Messenger, be on your way at this time.
Say to the renown King of Flesh,
And his council that is bound to him,
That they, make haste and come
As fast as they can ride.

Messenger [Sensuality]: My lord, I am your servant, Sensuality.
I am happy to carry your message.
You will see him very soon in your presence,
Your will, here, will be fulfilled.

---

92   Satan is referring to man taking the place of the fallen angels as God's favorites.

The stage of the Flesh

The Messenger, Sensuality, arrives. He goes to Flesh, thus saying:

Messenger: Hail, lord of the land, guided by sensuality!
Hail, Flesh in Lust, fairest to behold!
Hail, lord and leader of emperor and king alike!   400
The worthy World, by road and country way,
Has sent for you and your council.
Satan has assembled his household,
Awaiting your counsel and help.

Flesh: Hence, we will hasten to be there.
Let us no longer delay.

Messenger: You will bring happiness to their hearts;
By my truth, I safely say.

The stage of the World

Here comes the King of Flesh, attended by Lechery, Sloth, and Gluttony.

Flesh says to World
Flesh: Hail beloved and dear sovereign!
Why have you sent for me so hastily?

World: We are very glad to have you here,
To participate in our counsel!

Having ascended to the World's stage, they all seat themselves.

Now, Satan, tell us your plan.

Satan: Sirs, now that you are seated, I shall tell you:
Cyrus died the other day.
Now Mary, his daughter, that maid
Has been bequeathed his castle.

World: Certainly, sirs, I tell you,
If she may remain always in virtue,
She will be able to destroy hell,
Unless your council destroys her.

Flesh: Now you, Lady Lechery, you must attend her,
For you are the flower of fairest femininity.

You shall go and desire* to serve her and be her attendant,   *ask
For you shall most easily gain her confidence, you beryl of beauty.

Lechery: Sirs, I obey every aspect of your behest;
I will go straightway there at once.

Satan: Malignant spirits will come with you,
To help tempt her everywhere she goes.
Now that all seven are here,
Work craftily and win her favor.
Enter her person by the labor of Lechery,
So that she will finally come to hell.
Now you, malignant spirits, know what I mean.

The evil spirits emerge from hell

Bad angel: Sirs, I obey every aspect of your behest,
I will go straightway there at once.
Shhhhh, speak softly! I hasten to do her harm.
I pray you to hold your tongues.

The Castle of Magdalene

Here all the Seven Deadly Sins besiege the castle until Mary agrees to go to Jerusalem.

Lechery shall enter the castle with the Bad Angel.

Lechery: Hail Lady of most noble lineage!
Hail, [you are as] brilliant as the sun shining!
Many people are comforted by your benevolent trustfulness;
Your beauty beams brighter than the burnished sun,
Most debonair, angelic in demeanor!

Mary: Who are you that compliment me?

Lechery: One who wishes to be your servant.

Mary: Your debonair deference brings me into a rapture of tranquility.
Now, since it is your desire, for me to receive you into my service,
It would greatly please me.
You are heartily welcome to me.   450
Your speech is very amiable and imbued with reason.

Lechery: Now, good lady, will you tell me
Why you are not glad?

Mary: Because of my father, I have a heavy heart;
When I remember his death, I am overcome.

Lechery: Yes, lady, despite all that, be of good comfort.
Such heaviness can breed much distress,
Dispel such pains and deceptions,
Engage in pleasures that will please you.

Mary: In truth you are welcome in my presence,
Be my heart's leech.*   *healer
Brother Lazarus, if it pleases you,
And you sister Martha, to you both
I commend* this place into your governance,   *leave in your care
And commit you to God.

Lazarus: Now sister we shall do as you wish
[And] take up residence in this place
While you are absent,
To keep the place from disrepair.

Mary makes here way to Jerusalem with Lechery, and they go to a tavern.

A Tavern in Jerusalem

Taverner: I am a taverner, witty and wise,
That has a great many wines to sell.
Of all the taverners that dwell with the city,
I am the prize.
I have a great number of wines,
Both clear white and red:
Here is wine of Malta and malmsey
Clary wine, and claret, and many more,
Wine of the Netherlands, of Gaul, and made in Spain,
Wine of Guyenne and Italy, I say I have too.
You will find none better wherever you go.

Lechery: Lo, lady, comfort yourself and put yourself at ease.
Let us go there and have a taste;
This shall raise your spirits.
Taverner, bring us the finest you have.

Taverner: Here, lady is some wine, a repast,
That will well restore man and woman.
You will not think your money is wasted;
From cares and woe, it will relieve you.

Mary: Certainly, you say the truth, you are a good man,
Both courteous and kind to me.

A gallant, Curiosity, enters, and says:

Gallant: I am a fresh new gallant!
Beware the thirst, quench it!
Think you sirs that I am a merchant
Because I have just come to town?
With some pretty barmaid I would like to whisper.
I have a shirt from Raines with pendant sleeves,
And silk lace for my true lady [to admire].
Ah, how beautiful and resplendent she is!
When I am out of her presence, lord, how I sigh!
I will emulate sovereigns, and disdain commoners.   500
In winter, I will wear a waistcoat, in summer none at all;[93]
My doublet and hose always match.
I will be shaved before evening, so that I look young.
I have lovely locks of hair,
That makes me seem elegant and sexually appealing.
That's how I live in this word; I don't do it out of pride.

Lechery: Lady, as I can tell, at this time,
This is the man for you to talk to and occupy your time.

Mary: Call him in, taverner, and you will have my affection,
And we shall make merry, if he will come here.

Taverner: Hello, master Curiosity!

Curiosity: What do you want sir? What do you want with me?

Taverner: Here in my tavern is a gentlewoman, who desires your presence,
And to drink with you presently.

Curiosity: A dear duchess, a daisy's eye,*   *terms of endearment
[Dressed in] resplendent colors most feminine,
Your noble colors well arranged,[94]
Take my love, my allegiance,
Or I will be smitten with pains of perplexity [if you deny my advances].

---

93 He dresses fastidiously and fancies himself quite a catch. His name is interesting, in that a proper courtly lover would most likely be named Courtesy, while his name seems to be a play on that, as well as a warning that curiosity, especially in this case, can be dangerous. In line 550, we actually find out that it is the greatest of the seven deadly sins, Pride, that has disguised himself as the gallant.

94 Fine cloth and dyed fabrics are signs of wealth. He is probably also praising her fair skin and beauty.

Mary: Why sir, do you think I am a harlot?

Curiosity: No, princess, pardon me, you are my heart's healer.
If, by God, you will requite* my love!   *return

Mary: What causes you to love me so quickly?

Curiosity: Because I must my lady!
Your person, it is so womanly,
I cannot refrain, my sweet lily.

Mary: Sir, you are skilled in courtesy.*   *flattery

Courtesy: Now, gracious spirit, you are without peer.
I see you are of good breeding,*   *high estate/class
But will you dance with me, my dear?

Mary: Sir, I will happily agree.
You go first, I will follow you,
For a man ought to be respected at all times.

Curiosity: Now, by my faith, other matters grieve you,
Fill a cup, taverner! Let us have
Cups of wine [to cheer you up]. Yes, love?

Mary: As you will do, so will I.
I am very glad that we met;
I begin to fill with lust for you.

Curiosity: Now, darling dear, will you do as I advise?
We have drunk and eaten a little bread.
Will you go somewhere else* with me?   *insinuating his bedchamber

Mary: As you desire, my dear darling.
Though you go to the world's end,
I would never leave you.
I would die for your sake.

Mary and the Gallant leave. And the Bad Angel goes to the Stage.

The World, where the World, the Flesh, and the Devil are still gathered.

Bad Angel: Great largess* has befallen all you lords.   *bountiful gifts
You now have a fair and affable servant,
For she has fallen into our grisly claws.
Yes, Pride, called Curiosity, is dear to her;   550
He is most precious to her.
She has granted all he requests.
She finds his person very pleasing,
To her eyes, he is more pleasing than any king on a throne.

Satan: How I tremble and shake at these tidings!
Lechery, that noble servant that has tempted Mary into sin,
Go again, and be constantly Mary's guide.
Do not let her desist from the laudable life of lechery,
For her [fall], all hell shall rejoice.

The Bad Angel goes to Mary again.

Satan: At this time, I bid farewell to you two noble kings.
For I will now hasten to make my way home.
World: Farewell, Satan, prince of pride!

Flesh: Farewell, you who are best fit to make all sorrows cease!

> *Satan goes home to his stage, and Mary shall enter into the place alone,
> except for the Bad Angel. And all the seven Deadly sins shall convene at the house
> of Simon the Leper; they shall be arrayed like seven devils, and hide.*

The Place—an arbor that is the center acting area, representing Jerusalem, and surrounded by the other stages.

Mary will be in the arbor.

Mary: Ah, God be with my lovers,
My sweet birds, my loves so dear!
For they are the rewards for whom I am an amorous flower.
I am aggrieved that they are not here.
But I will rest in this arbor
Among these precious herbs,

Till some lover will appear
That desires to embrace and kiss me.
  Mary lies down and falls asleep the arbor.

The stage of Simon the Leper's house, a banquet is prepared.

Simon the Leper: This day I intend to entertain
My guests to the best of my ability.
I have ordered an abundant dinner
To cheer my best friends.
I will go into the city
To get provisions for my guests,
For the time draws near for the dinner,
And my servants are ready and have been given their orders.
I wish to God that I might make acquaintance
Of the Prophet* of true perfection,   *Jesus
Who will come to my place and feast!
It would bring joy to my heart and great gladness,
For reports of his high nobility
Spread throughout the country far and near.
His preaching is of great perfection,
Of righteousness and pure mercy.

The Place—Simon enters.

The Good Angel, sees Mary, as she still lies asleep in her arbor in one area of "the place."

Good Angel: Woman, woman, why are you so inconstant?
Full bitter is the cost of the bliss [you enjoy].
Why are you unable to remain faithful to God?
Do you believe that God made you for naught?
You have been enticed by sin and sorrow;
Fleshly lust has become delectable to you.
A salve for your soul must be found,
So that you may leave your vain and impure deeds.
Remember, woman, how that because of your poor pride,
Your soul shall lie in the fire of hell.
Remember how grievous it will be to abide
Forever in anger and resentment!

Think about mercy; make your soul pure. 600
I am the spirit of goodness that will guide you.

Mary: Ah, how the spirit of goodness hath inspired me at this time
And tempted me in the name of true perfection!
Alas, how bitterness does dwell in my heart!
I am enveloped in impure acts.
How dark thoughts did oppress me,
So that I sinned in every way.
O Lord, who shall save me from this despair?
Who shall be my spiritual guide to mercy?
I shall pursue the Prophet, wherever he may be,
For He is the fountain of perfect charity,[95]
He will heal me by the oil of mercy.
I will go and seek Him now with [my] sweet ointment,
And in every way, earnestly follow his commands.

The Place

Jesus enters with his disciples where they meet Simon and pass near Mary's arbor.

Simon: Now are you welcome master, most magnificent.
I humbly beseech You, that if You would be so gracious,
And if it be to the liking of your noble person,
Come and dine at my house this day.

Jesus: God of mercy, Simon, your hospitability is welcome!
I will enter your house with peace and fellowship.
I will gladly visit where grace can begin to grow.
For within thy house charity will reside,
And the beams of grace shall illuminate it.
Since you humbly offer me dinner,
With peace and grace, I shall enter your house.

Simon's house, at his stage

Simon: Master, most benign and gracious, I thank You,
That You, my Lord, most high
Will come to visit my house.
It is a great privilege for me.
Now sit down to the table, you masters all.

---

95 Charity comes from the word *caritas* and is God-directed love versus *amour* which is the flesh-based
love of one body for another.

They sit at the banquet.

Mary follows along and makes this lamentation:

Mary: Oh I, cursed wretch, who much woe hath wrought
Against my Maker most mighty!
I have offended Him in thought and deed.
But in his grace I place all my trust
Or else I know well that I am lost,
[My] body and soul are damned eternally.
Yet, good Lord of lords, my perennial hope,
You know my heart and thought well.
[That] is with Thee; I hope to stand in [God's] favor and grace.
Therefore, good Lord reward my heart's longing [for God].

Mary shall wash the feet of the Prophet with tears from her eyes,
wiping them with her hair, and then she anoints Him with a precious ointment.

Jesus says:

Jesus: Simon I give you special thanks
For the great feast that you have provided here.
But, Simon I will tell you this earnestly,
I have a few things to say to you.

Simon: Master whatever is your will,
And if it pleases You, I will listen.
Tell me what pleases You,
What your pleasure is and [what You] desire.

Jesus: Simon, there was a man in this present life
That had two debtors that owed him.   650
They were poor and could not repay him,
So they endured in debt.
The one owed a hundred pence to his guarantor,
And the other fifty, as it was.
And because he could not recover his money [from them],
They asked him to forgive the debt, and he forgave it.
So Simon, I pray you to answer this question for me:
Which of these two men was most beholding to that man?

Simon: Master, if it pleases You,
I reason that it is the man that owed him most.

Jesus: You have judged correctly. You are a wise man.
And have judged the question correctly.
If you can, examine your conscience,
You two are the debtors that I am referring to.[96]
Simon, behold this woman in every way;
How she weeps bitter tears,
And washes my feet and serves me,
And anoints them with ointments, kneeling low,
And with her fair, bright shining hair,
Wipes them demonstrating her good intentions.
Yet, since I have entered your house, Simon,
You did not offer to wash my feet
Or oblige me by wiping them.
In good conscience, you ought not reply.
But, woman, I say truthfully to you,
I forgive thee of thy sins,
And thereby your soul is made whole!

Mary: O blessed be Thou, Lord of everlasting life!
And blessed by thy birth by that pure virgin!
Blessed by Thou, food for my soul,
Medicine against the sickness of my soul!
And because I am guilty of the sin of pride,
I will clothe myself in humility
And oppose wrath and envy,
With the fair virtues of patience and charity.

Jesus: Woman, you are an expert in contrition,
And your soul has inward strength
And deserves future grace.
Your faith has saved you and made you shine spiritually.
Light has delivered you from darkness.
Therefore, I say to you, "depart in peace."

With this word, seven evils exit from Mary and the Bad Angel enters hell with thunder. [97]

Mary: Oh Thou glorious Lord! This had been done for my benefit;
Now my soul's health is restored.
Lord, because I despaired, I stand in dread,
Unless You bestow your mercy upon me.
You knew my thoughts without a doubt.

---

96   The two refers to Simon and Mary. Though Simon does not say anything here, Jesus discerns that Simon thinks that the true prophet would not let a woman of ill repute wash his feet.
97   Jesus has exorcised the demons from Mary.

Now may I trust in the teaching of Isaiah in the Scripture,
Whose reports of your nobility spread far and wide.

Jesus: Blessed are they always
That have not seen me and yet believe in me.   700
By your contrition, you have made recompense,
And saved thy soul from distress.*   *eternal damnation
Be on guard and do not fall into temptation,
And you will be my partner in eternal bliss.

    Jesus and his disciples leave, and the Good Angel rejoices over May Magdalene.

Good Angel: Holy God omnipotent,
I commend to your good governance [all mankind].
Humbly beseeching your imperial glory,
Let us be enwrapped in your divine virtue.
And delectable Jesus, wise sovereign,
Our faith we give into your care.
Most meekly we pray to your holy spirit,
Illuminate our ignorance with your divinity!
You are called Redemption, the soul's defender,

Which has been obscured by thy holy mortality.[98]
O true light, grant us your illumination,
So that we will not be seduced by the spirit of wrongdoing!
And Holy Spirit, to you most bounteous,
Three persons in the Trinity and one God eternal,
We consign our humble faith to you,
That we may come into your glorious bliss and escape sin;
We desire that you feed us with your spiritual food.

The stage of the Devil

Satan: Out, come up! I am incensed with hate!
I will hastily pass judgment,
I take issue with these beetle-browed ruffians.
Now, Belfagour, and Beelzubub, come see me!
    Two devils appear before their master [having come up out of hell].

2ⁿᵈ Devil: Here, lord! What do you want?

Satan: I am here to oversee the judgment of the rascals

---

98   Refers to Jesus' human incarnation and taking human form.

[Who are responsible for our lose of Mary] in my judicial role.
Now, thou Bad Angel, appear before me!
The Bad Angel appears and humbles himself.

Bad Angel: As flat as a fox, I fall before your face.

Satan: You rogue, what have you done wrong
That allowed this woman to break your bonds?

Bad Angel: The spirit of grace did sorely smite her
And tempted her greatly, that hypocrite!

Satan: You shall feel torment biting at your buttocks.
I will quickly avenge myself on you.

To his assistant devils

Come up, you devils, and whip him where he itches
And smear him with pitch!

Come on, you ruffians, see that it is done!
Here they beat all the Seven Deadly Sins as the did the first.

Satan: Now I have part of what I desire.
Now go into the house of hell, you louts,
And see that you set it on fire.
That will awake those within.

The other devils set the house of hell on fire and make fire rise from hell;
Mary goes to Lazarus and Martha.

Satan: So now have we frightened the inmates!
Their bodies and necks are burned.
Now let us also sink into hell,
With our black fellows.

They descend into hell.

The Castle of Magdalene, Bethany

Mary comes to Lazarus and Martha.

Mary: Oh brother, the blessed Prophet,
He who is matchless and blessed in life,
My heart's consolation and comfort,   750
Has made me clean and pleasing unto him.
This king, Christ, tended me, his creation.
I was drenched in various sins,
Till, by his power, the Lord healed me.
He would never deny me grace;
Though I was sinful, he said "turn again."
Oh, I, sinful creature, asked for grace,
And he healed me with the oil of mercy.

Martha: Now let the exalted name of Jesus be worshiped,
Which in Latin means Savior!
Fulfilling that title himself,
He is succor to the sinful and sick.

Lazarus: Sister, we welcome you into your tower.
I am glad to hear of your obsequiousness,
While I live, I will be honored to serve him
That has turned you from sin and irresolution.

Mary: Christ, who is the light and the clarity of day,
He has uncovered the darkness of the cloudy night,
[He] Who is the most true light of light,
Whose preaching is to us a gracious light:
Lord we beseech Thee, as You are the most mighty,
Out of the dead sleep of darkness defend us!
Give us the grace to forever rest consoled,
To quietly and peacefully serve You night and day!

Lazarus dies, saying:

Lazarus: Help, help sisters, for your love for me!
Alas death has set upon my heart!
Touch me! Where are you?
I falter and fall, I weaken from illness.
I feel a buzz in my head, all goes dark!
Good Jesus, be my guide!
I can no longer remain conscious!
I give up the ghost, I can no longer live!

Mary: O good brother take comfort,

And do not let heaviness dwell in your heart!
Let the faintness and fretting abate,
We shall fetch physicians to cure your pains.

Martha: I sigh, I am sorrowful, and say, "alas!"
This sorrow has been ordained to be my undoing.
Gentle sister, let us go quickly from this place.
The Prophet has great power in Him.
Good brother, take comfort,
We will go and seek your cure.

The Place

Mary and Martha meet with Jesus, as he is walking with his disciples.

Mary and Martha: O Lord Jesus, our most delectable sweetness,
Thou are the greatest, most glorious Lord,
Comfort your creature that cries to thee!
Behold your lover, good Lord,[99]
Lazarus lies sick and in great distress,
He loves you Lord, certainly.   800
Free him from his pains, good Lord.

Jesus: Of all infirmity, none can compare to death,
For all pains, it is impossible
To understand using reason. Even the most wise scholars
Cannot fathom the great works and joys
That are in the heavenly Jerusalem—
To see the joys of the Father in his glory,
The joys of the Son that ought to be praised,
The third person, the Holy Spirit,
All three in one, in heaven glorified.
Now you women that are in my presence here,
Take heed of my words:
Go home again to your brother Lazarus.
I shall send my grace to him.

Mary: We entreat you,
Thou glorious Lord, present upon earth,
We will be quickly upon our way.
Now, Lord, defend us from tribulation!

Mary and Martha go homeward, and Jesus leaves.

---

99 The language of "lover" is often used to in the Middle Ages to refer to ardent followers of Christ.

The Castle of Magdalene, Bethany

As they arrive, Lazarus is dying.

Lazarus: From despair, I am tossed like waves in the wind!
All hope is gone.
Death, death, thou art unkind!
My heart bursts! This is a sharp attack!
Farwell, my sisters, and my body's health!

He dies.

Mary: Jesus, my Lord be your succor,
He will be the treasure of your spirit!

Solider 1: God's grace will guide you
In everlasting joy!

Soldier 2: God divine, as it is in your power,
As he is one of the good souls, send him favor.

Martha: Now since it has befallen,
That death has dragged him down this day,
We must do our duties
And to the earth bring him without delay.

Mary: As is the custom now and always has been,
With weepers to the earth you must bring him.
All this must be done at I say to you—
While clad in black,* truly.   *wearing black in mourning

Soldier 1: Gracious ladies of great honor,
The people have come here into your sight,
Weeping and wailing with great sorrow,
Because of my lord's death.

> *A crowd of mourning neighbors joins the funeral procession from the
> Castle of Magdalene to the tomb in "the place." Here, one knight makes ready the
> stone and another brings in the weepers arrayed in black.*

Soldier 1: Now, all good friends that are present,
Take up this body gently
And lay it handsomely in his sepulcher for all to see.
Good Lord, save him from all ills!

They entomb him. The people then retire to the castle.
As he walks with his disciples in the "place," Jesus says:

Jesus: The time is come for true knowledge.
My disciples, come with me
To fulfill a petition,* as is in my power.   *request made of me
We go together into Judea;
There lies Lazarus, my friend.   850
We go together as the chosen people of the Light of God,
And we will save him from the grievous sleep of death.

Disciple: Lord, if it is your mighty will,
If he but sleeps, he can be saved through skill.[100]

Jesus: That is true, and it is possible;
By this, I will foreshadow my own death.
My Father, who is of exceeding charity,
Has sent me, his Son, to redeem mankind,
I, who was conceived by a pure virgin,
My mother, through clean incarnation;
And therefore I must suffer grievous Passion
Under Pontius Pilate, experience great distress,
Be beaten, mocked, scorned and crowned with thorns—
All this shall be the sufferance of my deity.
Therefore, follow me hastily,
To verify that Lazarus is indeed dead;
Wherefore I shall gladly show you that, as I say,
I had knowledge of his death, so that you can believe [in my miraculous power].

Jesus walks with his disciples toward the Castle of Magdalene, and one Jew tells
Martha:

Jew: Martha, Martha, be filled with gladness!
For as I say truly, the Prophet is coming
With his disciples, dressed in humility,
He shall comfort you with his mercy.

Martha runs toward Jesus, saying:

Martha: Lord, I am a simple creature, do not deny me,
Though I am wrapped in wretchedness!
Truly, Lord if Thou had been here,
I know he surely would not have died.

---

100 The apostle thinks that Jesus is referring to illness rather than death. Jesus' speech that follows makes
     it clear that he intends Lazarus' resurrection to prefigure his own, as well as to demonstrate his
     prophetic knowledge.

Jesus: Martha, daughter, I say unto you,
Thy brother will rise again.

Martha: Yes, Lord, on the last day;
That, I truly believe.

Jesus: I am the resurrection of life, that shall reign forever,
And whoever believes in me
Shall have life everlasting. That is the truth.
Martha, you believe this, truly?

Martha: Yes, truly, Prince of Bliss!
I believe in Christ, the Son of Wisdom,
Who will reign eternally
And redeem us frail beings from our sins.

Mary shall fall at Jesus's feet and say:

Mary: O Thou righteous regent, reigning justly,
Thou gracious Lord, Thou sweet Jesus!
Had Thou been here, my brother would be alive.
Good Lord, my heart does muse upon this.

Jesus: Where have you laid him? Tell me this.

Mary: He is in his tomb, Lord.

Jesus: Guide me to that place;
I desire to see that grave.

They lead Jesus to Lazarus' tomb.

Take away the stone of this grave!
Here, I will show you the covenant of grace.

Martha: Lord, your mandate shall be carried out:
I will remove this stone gladly.   900
Gracious Lord, I ask your mercy!
May your will be fulfilled here.

Martha removes the gravestone.

Jesus: Now Father, I beseech You of your divine paternity
That my prayer be favorable received by You, thy Fatherhood in glory.
Open your ears to thy Son living among humanity,
Not only for me, but truly for thy people,

That they may believe and receive thy mercy.
Father, for them I make supplication.
Gracious Father, grant me my boon!
Lazarus, Lazarus, come hither to me!

Lazarus: My Maker, my Savior, blessed be Thou!
Here men may know of thy miraculous works,
Lord, nothing is impossible for You.
For my body and my soul had departed from the world!
 I should have rotted, as does tinder;
My flesh should have dropped away from my bones.
Now what was laid asunder is lifted aloft to live again!
The goodness of God has done this for me,
For He is the remedy that can cure all woe,
That blessed Lord that has appeared here.

*All the people, the Jews, Mary, and Martha, with one voice say these
words: "We believe in you, Savior, Jesus, Jesus, Jesus."*

Jesus: I take heed of your good hearts,
Whereby I call you holy,
Between you and Me may there never be discord,
Therefore, I say, "Go in peace."

Jesus leaves with his disciples. Mary, Martha, and Lazarus return to the castle.

The stage of the King of Marseilles

The king and queen are present. The King of Marseilles gives a speech:

King: Out of the way unworthy wretches!
Why do you not bow low to my laudable presence?
You brawling ruffians, and blabber lipped bitches,
Why do you not obediently do my will without offending me?
I am a handsome sovereign, unmatched,
There is no such another under the sun, to tell the truth.
When I ride fresh and fierce onto the field,
My foes flee from the fray.
I am honored like an emperor.
When banners begin to blaze and trumpets begin to blow,
I am held highest of sovereigns in all heathendom.
Kings and emperors will acknowledge me
Or else they pay sorely for their boldness.
I am King of Marseilles, truly let it be told;
I will have it known far and near,

Who would say the contrary, I will make him suffer.
I have a pleasing wife, fresh as a falcon;
She is fair and feminine.
When I look on this lady, I am as lusty as a lion.
In my sight,
Of sensual delight,
Of felicitous companionship,
Of all wives most pleasing,
[She is] my bliss, my beauty bright!

Queen: Most noble and honorable,   950
Humbly I thank you for commending me.
You most bounteous and boldest [man] under the bright banner of war,
No creature so magnificent can bring me such comfort.
Your presence renews me.
Your prowess protects me from all dangers.
For you, I keep myself pure.
To please your person, brings me joy.

King: Oh my god! Brightest beryl of beauty,
Ruby ruddy as a rose,
You are so pleasing to me that you put my cares to flight.

To his knights

Now comely knights, prepare and bring
Spices and wine here quickly.

The knights get spices and wine.

On the stage of hell, a devil enters in horrible garb.

Devil: Out, out, leave! I will cry and yell,
For our labor is wasted, therefore I say alas!
Of all the prisons most painful, none is so [fortified] as hell,
[Yet] our iron bars and strong gates of brass are burst asunder![101]
The King of Joy has entered therein, as bright as fire's blaze;
For fear of his fearful banner, our fellowship has fled away.
When He touched the gates, at his touch they burst like glass.
The roof split, as if by thunder.
Now we are thralls, that previously were free,

---

101 The Harrowing of Hell and the rescue of the Old Testament patriarchs.

[Made so] by the Passion of Christ
On a cross on high, He was hanged,
That has destroyed our labor and all our deeds.
He has emptied Limbo and guided them to paradise.
That wondrous deed has injured us:
Adam and Abraham, and all their kin,
Out of our prison to joy they were taken.
All this has been done since noon Friday:
He has broken through our gates that hung high.
Now He is risen, his resurrection has happened,
And He is on his way to Galilee.
We tried to entice Him with many a temptation,
To test whether He was God or not.[102]
Yet for all our efforts, we were deceived,
For with his fantastic deeds, He has rescued every one of them.
Now for all eternity,
None will fall into our clutches,
Unless He deems it so,
By his righteous judgment
And judicious governance.
This I tell you all, and in conclusion, I return to hell.
　　He goes down to hell.

The Place

Enter the three Marys dressed as chaste women, with signs of the Passion printed on their breasts.

Mary Magdalene: Alas, alas, for that royal beam of light!
This has pierced my heart worst of all:
Here, He turned once again to the woman of Jerusalem,
And out of weariness, let the cross fall.

Mary Jacobe: This sorrow is more bitter than any:
For the Jews struck Him to make him go on,
Showing their spite for the royal king.
That cleaves my heart and fills me with woe.[103]   1000

Mary Salome: It is intolerable to see and tell,
To see that oppressive torment visited on any creature.

102　Alludes to Christ's temptation in the wilderness.
103　The blame placed on the Jews for their treatment of Christ is one of the sources of anti-Semitism. This emphasis is found in the Gospel of John.

O Lord that had endured incredible strife!
It is too hideous to tell.

At this the Marys with one voice say the following:

Marys: Hail, glorious cross! Thou bore that Lord on high,
Which by thy might did lowly bow down,
To redeem man's soul from servitude,
That otherwise would have endured the pains of hell forever.
As recorded by of David in resolute voice,
"Lord bow down your heavens, and descend."[104]

Mary Magdalene: Now let us go to the tomb,
Where our Lord and Savior was laid,
To anoint Him, body and bone,
To make amends for our trespasses.

They proceed to the grave.

Who shall lift the lid of the tomb,
That we may anoint his gracious wounds,
With precious balms, this hour
As we intend, to show our loving devotion?

Mary Salome: That blissed body within the bonds of this tomb,
Was laid here with rueful moans;
Never creature was born upon this earth
That has ever suffered such hideous wounds.

Two angels in white appear at the grave.

Angel 1: You women present, be not afraid.
Jesus is risen and is not here.
Lo, here is the place that He was laid.
Go see, He will appear to Peter and his disciples.

Angel 2: In Galilee, without a doubt,
You shall see Him, as he said.
Go your way and take comfort and be of good cheer.
For that which He foretold shall no longer be delayed.

The angles leave; the Marys return from the tomb. The Marys meet Peter and John.

---

104 Psalms 144:5.

Mary Magdalene: O Peter and John, we are beguiled.
Our Lord's body has been borne away!
I am afraid it has been defiled.
I am so distressed; I don't know what to say.

Peter: These tidings greatly dismay me!
I will hurry there with all speed.
Now, Lord defend us as best you can!
We will go look in his sepulcher.

John: My soul, which should guide my body,
Is in great distress,
When I remember
The torment, the wide wounds, my Lord endured!

Peter: That suffering and pain He endured
For our offenses and sins.
And I forsook Him for all his torments,[105]
I took no heed of his teachings and exhortations.

Peter and John go to the tomb, and the Marys follow.

Peter: Now I see and know the truth!
Gracious Lord, protect us!
There is nothing left here but a shroud
That is testament to thy burial.   1050

John: I am afraid of wicked oppression;
What has become of Him, I cannot discern.
But He said that after the third day He would be resurrected.
This was prophesied long ago.

The disciples leave Mary Magdalene alone by the tomb. She stands apart from the other Marys.

Mary Magdalene: Alas! I may no longer live,
For the sorrow and misery that dwell in my heart.

An angel appears.

Angel 1: Woman, woman, why do you weep?
Whom do you seek in such sadness?

---

105 Refers to Peter's denying being one of Christ's apostles, three times, after his death.

Mary Magdalene: I wish that I knew
Who hath borne away my Lord Jesus.

Jesus appears. Mary mistakes him for a gardener.

Jesus: Woman, woman, why do thou weep?
Who do you seek in such sadness?

Mary Magdalene: Good sir, tell me now,
If you have borne away my Jesus,
For I intended in every way
To have Him with me,
Who has been my one true Lord,
And I am his loving follower and his mission is dear to me.[106]

Jesus: Mary!

Mary Magdalene: Gracious Master and Lord, it is You that I seek!
Let me anoint You with these sweet balms.
You have long been hidden from me,
But now I will kiss Thee, who are my heart's remedy.

Jesus: Touch me not, Mary. I have not yet ascended
To my Father in heaven, and out of your realm;
Go tell my brothers that I intend
To ascend to my Father in his heavenly towers.

Mary Magdalene: Truly, when I first saw you, Lord,
I thought you were Simon the gardener.

Jesus: Truly, so I am, Mary:
Man's heart is my garden on earth.
Therein, I sow seeds of virtue all the year;
The foul weeds and vines, I rend up by the root;
When the garden is watered with clean tears,
Then spring up the virtuous, sweetly scented.

Mary Magdalene: Thou dear worthy emperor, thou great divinity!
To me this is joyful news,
And will be to all people that live after us.
When they know that it is possible,
This knowledge of your divinity
Will be joyfully embraced.

---

106 His mission or cause it to bring people to the true faith. This may also foreshadow Mary's role in
converting Marseilles.

Jesus: I will appear to sinners, as to you,
If they will seek me with fervent love
And be steadfast, I will always be with thee,
And with all those who meekly come to me.

*Jesus leaves suddenly, as Mary Magdalene joins the other Marys,
She says:*

Mary Magdalene: Sisters, with the high and noble overflowing grace,
My most blessed Lord Jesus, Jesus, Jesus,
Appeared to me at the tomb when I was there!
He relieved my sorrow and elevated me to bliss,
That is too great to express   1100
Or for any one tongue to tell.
My joy is great,
Far exceeding my pain!

Mary Salome: Now let us go to the city of Our Lady dear,
To tell her of his state
And the disciples too, as we have seen it here,
That they may rejoice and be healed of their despair.

Mary Jacobe: Now sister Magdalene, with good cheer,
Would that we might meet with the good Lord!

Jesus reappears

Jesus: To show hearts that desire me that I am near,
I appear to you, women, and say "fare you well!"

Mary Salome: Now gracious Lord, of your exceeding charity—
Grant us, who grieve in your presence with humble hearts,
Your divine blessing
To spiritually sustain our souls.

Jesus: All are blessed who can refrain from sorrow.
We bless you, Father, Son, and Holy Ghost,
Who can constrain your sorrow and care.
In the name of the Father, the Son, and the Holy Spirit, amen!

Go you to my brethren and say to them there
That if they proceed into Galilee,
There they shall see me, as I said earlier,
In body with their physical eyes.

Jesus disappears again.

Mary Magdalene: O Thou, glorious Lord of heaven's realm,
Now blessed by thy divinity
That appeared incarnate
To visit thy three poor servants.
Thy will, gracious Lord, shall be fulfilled.
All things will be done as Thou command us.
We will go see our gracious brethren,
And tell them of our joy in seeing You.

Marys leave.

The king, at his stage, is attended by his queen and followers.

The King of Marseilles begins a sacrifice.

King of Marseilles: Now lords and ladies of great worth,
I urge you to attend a religious observance
This day to offer sacrifice
With a multitude of mirth, before all our gods.
Offer sincere prayers in [Mohammad's] presence
Every man with somber heart.

Queen: To that courteous and kind lord,
Mohammad, that is so great of might
With music and mirth in mind,
Let us make an offering in that high king's sight.

They start off for the temple.

The stage of the heathen temple in Marseilles

A heathen priest and his boy enter.

Priest: Now, my clerk, Hawkin, for love of me
See to it that my altar is arrayed.*   *prepared or readied
Go ring a bell or two or three.
Quickly child, do not delay,
For here shall be a religious ceremony.
Look, boy, that you do it hastily.

Boy: What, master would thou have your wench do in your bed?
Thou will have to wait until I've sung my service.*   *had my turn in bed with her
1150

Priest: Boy, I say, by Saint Coppin,
I spoke no such words to you.

Boy: Whether you did or not, the first ride upon her shall be mine,
For, by my faith, thou are burdened;
My sire, great master Morell,
For you have so filled your belly with gruel
That it grows as great as the devil out of hell.
You are unshapely* to look upon.   *fat and grotesque
When women come to hear your sermon,
I can sweetly make love with them—

[Ladies like] Kirchon and fair Marion.
They love me better than you.
I dare say, if you should ride upon them,
Your body is so great and wide,
That no horse can hold you,
Unless you broke its back.

Priest: Thou lie, by the devil of hell!
I pray that the god Mohammed kill you!
I shall whip thee until your buttocks roar,
I will perform miracles [of whipping] on your arse.

Boy: A fart, master, and kiss my groin!
The devil of hell was thy uncle.

To the audience.

Masters, the stock from which [my master] came,
Lately sprung from the devil's loins.

Priest: Mohammed's blood, precious knave!
You will have stripes on your ass
And raps on the head!

Beats him.
Arriving at temple, the king says:

King: Now priest and clerks of this holy temple,
Let me see you sing your service.

Priest: Yes sovereign lord, we shall do out duty.
Boy, bring a book quickly!
Now boy, I will prepare myself for service at the altar.
Put my vestments and attire on me.

Boy: Now I will read the lesson.
Such as is appropriate for the day:

"Lectio Mahowndis, viri fortissimo Sarasenorum,[107]
Glabriosum ad glumandum glumardinorum,
Gormondorum alocorum, stampatinantum cursorum,
Cownthtes fulcatum, congruriandum tersorum,
Mursum malgorum, Mararagorum,
Skartum sialporum, fartum cardiculorum,
Slaundri stroumppum, corbolcorum,
Sniguer snagoer werwolfforum
Standgardum lamba beffettorum,
Strowtum stardi strangolcorum,
Rigor dagor flapporum,
Castratum ratirybaldorum

Hounds and hogs in hedges and hills,
Snakes and toads must be your lovers;
May the devils, Ragnell and Roffin and others,   1200
Grant you the grace to die on the gallows."

Priest: Now lords and ladies, of lesser and greater rank,
Kneel down with great devotion.
Young and old, rich and poor,
Make your offering to Saint Mohammed,
And you shall have his great pardon,
That can be found in this holy place,
And you will receive my blessing
And stand in Mohammed's grace.

   The king kneels and says,

King: Mohammed, you are the most mighty,
A glorious ghost in my sight.
You comfort me in country and on the shore*   *everywhere
With thy wisdom and thy wit;
For truly, lord, I trust in you.
Good lord, do not let my soul be lost!
You know my innermost thoughts.

---

107 This incantation is Latin gibberish, beginning with the line, '*The Book of Mohammed*, most mighty
    men of the Saracens . . .'

I kneel in thy presence,
This gold coin, rich and round,
I offer it to you for my lady and me,
That you will be our comfort in this hour.
Sweet Mohammed remember me!

Priest: Now boy, I pray thee, let us hear a song,
Let us sing the service, I say.
Swell thy breast, stand not too long,
And start this day's service.

Boy: I hum what I may
With merry tune, I sing the treble.

Both sing.

Priest: Hold on, the devil frightens you,
If you do not do things as I have ordered.
Now, sir king, queen and knight,
Be merry in heart everyone,
For you may see bright relics here:
Mohammed's own neck bone,
And you shall see it pass before you,
No matter what happens to you,
And you shall kiss this holy bone
Mohammed's own eyelid.
You shall know its great value,
And its power:
It can make you blind forever,
This holy bead.*   *eye
Lords and ladies, old and young,
The worthy Mohammed, and the dear dragon,
And the good Goliath, bring you everlasting bliss,
That you may sing in joy
Before that beauteous king
That is god of us all.

They withdraw.

Pilate comes onto his stage with attendants.

Pilate: Now good sergeants, what say you?
You are wise men knowledgeable in law.   1250
I need to know about the death of Jesus,
And our sovereign Caesar also needs to know the truth.
This Jesus was a man of great virtue,
And had worked many wonders in his time.
He was put to death by unjust accusations,
Which sticks in my mind.
You know well how He was buried in the earth,
Guarded by knights with great weapons.
Yet, He has risen again, as He foretold,
And Joseph of Arimethea has taken Him away.[108]

Sergeant 1: Sovereign judge, all that you say is true.
And all this must be subtly dealt with.
We must say that his disciples took Him;
This will be the answer to which I will attest.

Sergeant 2: That seems most likely to be true;
Your council is good and commendable.
So write a special epistle Caesar
That is most likely to profit us.

Pilate: Now messenger, come hither in haste!
You must deliver a message that I have written,
To the sovereign emperor of Rome.
But first go to King Herod,
And say that I am sending him knowledge
Of Christ's death and how it was achieved.
I charge you with delivering this message and do not tarry
Until the letter has been brought to the emperor.

Pilate's Messenger: My lord, I will hasten to deliver you message
To that lord of royal renown.
Do not doubt that it shall indeed be done,
Hence will I make my way quickly out of this town.

---

108 Joseph of Arimethea is said to have brought the Holy Grail to England. Lancelot and Galahad are his
     descendants. Galahad, the last of his line, achieves the Grail quest.

The messenger goes to Herod and
his attendants at his stage.

Messenger: Hail, sovereign crowned king!
The princes of the law commend themselves to your royal highness,
And send you tidings of Christ's Passion,
And this letter tell you the details.

Herod: By my truth, now I am full of bliss!
These are merry tidings of what they have accomplished.
Certainly, I am glad of this;
Now, we are friends that before were foes.
Wait for a reward, messenger, and then be gone,
And recommend me to your sovereign's grace.

Tell him I will be his steadfast supporter,
Far and near and in every place.

The messenger goes to the emperor
and his attendants at his stage.

Messenger: Hail to you, sovereign, sitting in grace!
Hail, worthy one without peer!
Hail, great governor capable of granting all grace!
Hail, emperor of the world both far and near!
Sovereign, if it pleases your high authority,
I have brought you a letter of great worth
From Pilate, your high judge,
Which you will see fulfills your desire.   1300
He sent you word, a humble declaration,
That he has kept your decrees,
As he is bound by his office.

Emperor: Welcome, messenger bearing good news!
Let me see the letter.

Takes the letter

My judges, give your attention
To understand what this letter says—
Whether it be good [news], or mischance,
Or else of no help to me,
Let me know quickly.

Provost: Sir, we will peruse the content,
To see if it is pleasing to your excellence.
The intent of this epistle is thus:
Pilate commends himself to you,
And the message is about a Prophet,
Whose name is Jesus.
He was put to death violently,
Because He claimed to be the King of the Jews,
Also He claimed He himself was Son of the Godhead;
Therefore, He was crucified until He was dead
And afterwards buried, so they thought.
The third night his body was treacherously stolen;
His disciples are so devoted to Him,
That they took Him away.
I marvel how they managed the decaying body,
I expect they were greeted with a perverse food.[109]

Emperor: They were crafty, truth to tell.
This epistle I will keep with me, if I can;
I will have the year and reign chronicled,
That it shall never be forgotten by whoever looks upon [the books].
Messenger, leave this town with haste!
Take this gold as your wage,
Merrily made.

Messenger: Farewell, my lord of great renown,
I will make my way out of this town.

They all withdraw.

Mary Magdalene enters with the disciples, and says:

Mary Magdalene: Now, I remember my Lord that was put to death
By the Jews, though he was without guilt and did no treason.
The third night, He rose by the might of his Godhead:
On Sunday was his glorious resurrection,
And now, in the time since He has gloriously ascended;
He has ascended into heaven, and there He is king.
His great kindness cannot leave my remembrance.
Of all different tongues, He gave us knowing.[110]
Now the disciples have taken passage

---

109 Unintended pun on the Provost's part, since the body of Christ is the Eucharist.

110 This is the gift of languages given to the disciples at Pentecost so that they can convert people throughout the world to Christianity. Mary will now, like the apostles, take up that mission and go to Marseilles and covert its king and queen. This becomes the legend of Mary Magdalene converting Provence.

To diverse countries here and far beyond,
To preach and teach of his Passion;
My brethren have dispersed and gone far away.

She stands aside.

Heaven opens and Jesus shows himself.

Jesus: O, uneclipsed sun, the temple of Solomon,[111]
I rested in a perfect moon that never waxed nor waned,   1350
A ship for Noah, a fleece of Gideon.
She was my tabernacle of great nobility;
She was the palace of Phoebus bright;
She was the vessel of pure cleanness,
Where my Godhead was made man.
My blessed mother, my gracious femininity,
Mankind's defense from the fiend,
Queen of Jerusalem, the heavenly city,
Empress against hell.
She is precious incense,
The precious cinnabar that purges the body;
She is the musk against epilepsy,
The gentile gillyflower against attacks of the heart.
No tongue can fully express the goodness of my mother;
No clerk can [ever] write well enough of her joys.
But now I turn with kindness to my servant [Mary Magdalene],
With a heavenly message, I intend to visit her.

He turns to the angel Raphael

Raphael, my angel, present here in my sight,
Now descend to Mary Magdalene.
Bid her, in accordance with my will, she cross the sea,
And tell her that she shall convert Marseilles.

Angel: O glorious Lord, I will go
And show your servant your grace.
She shall work for that land's spiritual comfort,
And redeem them from pagan wretchedness.

Then the angel descends and appears to Mary.[112]

---

111 This is Jesus' metaphoric praise of the Virgin Mary (1349-65). At this point in the play, Jesus is inviting comparison between the Blessed Virgin and Mary Magdalene, which reaches its acme in the ascension into heaven at the end of the play.

112 Parallels the Annunciation, Gabriel to the Virgin, though here Mary is sent to France to convert a people, echoing the mission given the apostles at Pentecost.

Be not abashed, Mary, in this place!
Our Lord gives you a commandment that you must fulfill,
To pass over the sea in a short time
To the land of Marseilles.
You shall convert the king and queen,
And be received as a holy apostle.
By you alone, all the land shall be taught.
You shall teach them God's laws.
Therefore, go forth in gladness
To fulfill God's commandment.

Mary: He that made the seven devils flee from my person,
Through his virtue, all things are possible!
I am ready to go forth to those people.
As you have commanded, they shall be brought into virtue.*   *the true faith
With thy grace, good Lord divine,
Now I will hastily go to the sea
And secure passage.
Now speed me, Lord in eternal glory!
I will make haste, almighty Trinity!

    A ship enters the place with a merry song.

Shipmaster: Strike, Strike! Lower the sails to the ground.
Here I see a fair haven.
Let us measure the depth to make sure.
I hope we have found a good harbor.
You boy, look that we have libations!

Boy: I have not done that because I'm sleepy, but I swear by God,   1400
That you would have to wait for it, even if you were my father.

Master: Why are we not ready to go to dinner, boy?
Shall we not have any food?

Boy: You will not have any good cheer by my doing!
Though you be so hungry that you were ravenous,
I told you this plainly before!
I have such a cramp coming on me,
[That] I am about to take a turn for the worse;
I lie and twist about till I piss,
And am almost destroyed!

Shipmaster: Now, boy, what do you want now?

Boy: Nothing but a fair damsel,
Could help me, I know it well,
Or else I may rue the day that I was born.[113]

Master: By my truth, boy you shall be healed.
I will bring one into your bed!
Now shall you learn to wed a damsel;
She will kiss you and teach you a lesson.[114]

He raises a whip and beats him.

Boy: Don't hit me; I will be serious!
May the devil make your head burst,
For all my courage is now gone!
Alas, I am forlorn!

Mary steps forward.

Mary: Shipmaster, a word with you.

Shipmaster: Certainly, fair woman, what do you need?

Mary: Where is your ship going? Tell me that,
And if you will sail shortly.

Shipmaster: We will sail this same day,
If the wind is in our favor.
This ship that I speak of
Sets sail for the land of Marseilles.

Mary: Sir may I sail with you?
You will have payment.

Shipmaster: You will not lack passage,
For the wind is good and safe for us.

Mary boards, and they set sail.

Yonder is the land of Turkey;[115]
I would be loath to lie to you.

---

113 The shipmaster and the boy, like the priest and his boy, provide comic relief much like the gravediggers in *Hamlet*. Here the boy's pains and appetite are not physical but signify carnal desire.
114 The shipmaster puts an end to the boy's lusty fantasies by beating him.
115 The captain points landmarks out to Mary as they sail. By the end of his speech, they have reached Marseilles.

Now the shipmen sing.

We need not worry about our course.
Yonder in the land of Satalia.*   *Asia Minor
Strike! Beware of sand!
Take a sounding and guide us in.
This is the land of the King of Marseilles.
Now disembark, thou fair women,
[And go] to the king's place; you can see it in the distance.

She disembarks.

Cast off, cast off from the land!

Boy: All ready, master, at your command!

The ship goes out of the place.

Mary: O Jesus, thy sweet name
Must be reverently worshipped!
Lord grant me victory against the fiend's flame,
And allow me to convert these people to your laws.[116]
I go forth with great dedication [to that cause];   1450
I will enter into the king's presence,
And teach him the meaning of my Lord's laws
And of his Godhead and his power.

The stage of the king of Marseilles

Mary enters to have an audience with the king.

Now, the high king Christ, man's redemption,
May save you, sir king, reigning in equity,
And guide you on the way to salvation!
Jesus, the son of the mighty Trinity,
That was and is and every shall be,
For man's soul the reformation,
In his name, lord, I beseech thee,
To let me reside within this land.

King: Jesus? Jesus? What devil is he? Who?
I defy you and your opinion.

---

116 Laws signifies Christianity.

Thou false reprobate, I shall flatten you.
Who made you so bold to appear so insolent [before me]?

Mary: Sir, I do not come to deceive you.
The good Lord Christ has compelled my journey here.
[So that you] receive Him as your spiritual nourishment,
And thy former erroneous faith is effaced by Him.

King: And what is that lord that you speak of here?

Mary: It is the Savior, if you will learn [of Him],
The second person, that did conquer hell,
And the Son of the Father in the Trinity.

King: And what power does that god have that you tell me about?

Mary: He made heaven and earth, land and sea,
And all this He made out of nothing.

King: Woman, I pray you answer me:
What did God make in the very beginning?[117]
We would [like to] understand this,
It would please me to learn.

Mary: Jesus, mercy!
Sir, I will declare all and some,
That God first created.
He said, "In the beginning was the Word,"
And with that He proved his great Godhead.
He made heaven for our aid,
Where He sits on a high throne;
His ministers next, as He saw the need—
His angels and archangels, all the company—
God made all this on the first day,
As was pleasing to Him.
On Monday, He did not forget
To make the sun, moon, and stars and the firmament—
The sun (was made) to begin its course in the orient [in the east],
And ever labor without weariness,
And keep its course to the occident [and set in the west].

---

117 It is common in conversion stories and elsewhere that educating people about God's supreme power
begins with the story of Creation. In England, this tradition goes back to "Caedmon's Hymn."
Caedmon was a lowly man who felt badly because he could not sing a story like others at a feast. He
leaves, and is visited by an angel, who divinely inspires him to "sing the Creation," now known as
"Caedmon's Hymn." Once his song is heard, he is invited by an abbess to become a monk, who was
thereafter sought out for the songs he sung and taught celebrating God and Scripture.

On Tuesday, as I understand it,
Further riches he created for us:
That day He set about making the waters,
As was pleasing to his goodness.   1500
As Scripture bears witness,
At that time, He made both sea and land,
All that was the work of his great nobility,
Pleasing for Him to ordain.
On Wednesday, our Lord of might
Made more as it pleased him:
Fish in the waters and fowl in flight—
And all that was to aid mankind.
On Thursday, that noble king
Made different beasts, great and small;
He gave them earth to feed them,
And made them multiple throughout every hill and dale,
And on Friday, God made man,
In his own likeness,
As it pleased his divinity,
And breathed the Holy Ghost* into them.   *life
On Saturday, as I will tell you,
He blessed all his works;
He bade them to multiple and increase,
As was pleasing to Him in his worthiness.
And on Sunday He rested,
As Scripture plainly declares,
That day all should worship Him,
Their maker who sustains them—
Sunday is for offering Him devotion,
And Him alone, as I have plainly told you.

King: Hark, woman, you have many great reasons,
But I think, these things were the work of my gods!
But unless you can answer me immediately, I shall torture you
And cut your tongue out of your head!

Mary: Sir, if I said something amiss, I would recant it.
Leave the bonds of your troubled state of mind,
And tell me who your gods are,
And how they have saved us from tribulation.

King: Hence, let us go to the temple,
And there you shall see a solemn sight.
Come all of both high and low position,
And observe my god's might on this day.

The king and all his attendants go to the temple, where the heathen priest and his clerk await them.

The king points to the idols.

Look now, what do you say about this sight?
See how pleasantly they stand!
Lord, I beseech your great might,
Speak to this Christian that you see here.
Speak good lord, speak! See how I bow!
Hark, thou priest, what does this mean?
What? Speak good lord, speak! What ails you now?
Speak, since you are the source of all bliss!

Priest: Lord, he will not speak while the Christian is here.

Mary: Sir king, if it pleases your gentleness,
Give me license to make my prayers
To my God in heaven's bliss,   1550
And [ask him] to show you a miracle for your sake.

King: Pray until your knees ache!

Mary: The lord is my light;* who shall I fear?   *salvation
"The Lord is the protector of my life; of whom shall I be afraid?"[118]

The idol trembles and quakes.
Now, Lord of lords, to thy blissful name sanctified
I most meekly entrust my faith,
Destroy the pride of false idols!
Lord, let thy goodness descend to thy lover;*   *faithful follower
Do not let their pride presume against your divinity,
Where thy name is uttered Jesus!
Good Lord, I faithfully offer my prayer:
Lord, reveal thy righteousness!

A cloud descends from heaven and sets the temple on fire. The priest and clerk sink into the ground.

The king goes home, saying:

King: Damn, I have been deluded!
I will be avenged for my cruel turmoil!
Alas, the might of my gods has been disproven to me.

---

118 Psalms 27:1

To Mary:

Thou woman, come closer and learn what I have to say:
My wife and I have been together many years,
And never have been able to conceive a child.
If thou can find a means to accomplish this,
I will obey thy God, and to Him humbly submit.[119]

Mary: Now sir, since you have said this,
I will rightfully beseech my Lord.
Believe in Him and in no other,
And I hope she shall conceive soon.

King: Leave, Leave! I am getting ill!
I will go to bed at once.
I am so taken with sickness,
I feel near death!

    The king goes to bed quickly.

    And Mary goes to a dilapidated hut, standing outside, she says:

Mary: Now Christ, my creator, keep and protect me,
That I may not be confounded by this rebuke!
I cry to Thee for hunger and thirst;
Lord deal with me judiciously!
As Thou saved Daniel from the fierce lion,
By Habakkuk, your messenger, who brought him sustenance,
Good Lord, help and succor me,
As is thy divine pleasure, Lord!

    Christ, in heaven, speaks to his angels.

Jesus: My grace shall grow and descend
To Mary, my lover, that has called me
To rectify her condition.
Her need for corporal sustenance shall be relieved.
Now angels, descend to her,
Lead her right to the prince's chamber
And precede her with divine light.
Tell her to ask him to voluntarily share his wealth.

---

119 The king makes a demand, a child (a miracle), for his conversion. When Mary says she cannot make
such a promise, he sends her away. She stays in a rundown hovel and has little to sustain her. Mary
also represents the poor and downtrodden at this point.

Angel 1: Blessed Lord, we will descend to Mary,
As you will be able to see.

Angel 2: We descend from your bright bliss;
We carry out your commandment.

The angels descend. The first says:

Angel 1: Mary, our Lord will send you comfort:
He commands you to make your way to the king,   1600
To test him and ask him if he will make concessions.
While he is sleeping, test him.

Angel 2: Ask him to deliver you from your distress to satisfy God.
We will go in front of you with solemn light;
We will be dressed in mantles of white.
The doors shall rightly open before us.

Mary: O gracious God, I understand!
This white clothing betokens meekness.
Now, gracious Lord, I will not refuse
To humbly obey your command.

Mary goes with the angels bearing lights before her to the king's bed, she says:

Thou wayward king, troubled and mad,
That has all the wealth of the world at thy will,
Give me some of thy goods,
For I hunger, thirst, and am cold!
God has sent you many warnings:
I advise you to be converted.
Fear your wickedness, for your own spiritual health!
And, you queen, relinquish your worldly goods.

Mary leaves, and the angels and Mary change out of their white clothing.

King: The day has come! I am merry and glad;
The sun is up and shines brightly.
I had a marvelous vision in my sleep
That has sorely trouble me, this night:
I saw a fair woman,
All clad in white;
She was led by angels bright;
She gravely spoke words to me.

Queen: I believe they were sent from God!
We may have doubts in our hearts [about our ways].
I thought our chamber should have burned
From the lights there all about!
She spoke words of warning to us,
That we should help those that are in need
By sharing our wealth, as God bids—
I say without doubt!

King: Now, good wife, you say quite rightly.

The king summons a soldier.

A knight come quickly!

A soldier approaches.

Now, as you are true as steel,
Go fetch that woman that appeared to me [yesterday].

Solider: My sovereign lord, I will go on my way;
She shall come, as it pleases you.
I will go tell her what your sovereign wishes.
It is an act of charity to help her.

The soldier crosses the stage to Mary.

Good health, good woman! I have been sent
To fetch you to speak to the king.

Mary: Gladly, sir, as he wishes.
I will come since it pleases him.

Mary crosses the stage to the king.

May the might and power of the Holy Trinity,
And the wisdom of the Son, govern you rightly!
The Holy Ghost be with you!
What is your will? Tell me directly.   1650

King: Thou fair woman, it is my delight
And my intent to provide for you,
With food and money, and clothes for the night,
With the wealth that God has endowed me.

Mary: Then you will be fulfilling God's commandment,
Giving sustenance to poor people who are in distress.

King: Now blessed women, recite here
The joys of your Lord in heaven.

Mary: Blessed be the hour, blessed be the time,
That you will believe in God's laws!
You will make a new beginning,
Against the fiend's malfeasance.
From God above comes the grace
Now set in your breast by the Holy Ghost,
To make amends for your sins
And bring your soul to everlasting salvation.
Your wife, she is great with child;
As thou desired, thou hast thy boon.

Queen: Yes, I feel it stir, moving up and down in my womb!
I am glad you have come into our presence.
O blessed women, root of our salvation,
I will worship thy God with the reverence He is due.

King: Now fair women, tell me truly,
I beseech you: what is your name?

Mary: Sir, I will not resist telling you,
Mary Magdalene, without a doubt.

King: O blessed Mary, I feel graced
By the actions I have taken this day.
Now I thank God, and you especially,
And will do so for the rest of my life.

Mary: You shall go to Peter, without delay, and thank him for [your new faith].
He is thy friend, steadfast and pure;
He has helped me pray to almighty God,
And he shall christen* you, protecting you from the fiend's power   *baptize
In the sight of God on high.

King: Your answer surely delights me;
I am very glad of these tidings.
Mary, I give you this day, all my property and wealth
To be governed by you;
You will rule all as you please,
Until I come home again.

I will not ask of you neither land nor payment,
Rather, I give you full power over all.

Queen: Now, worshipful lord, a boon I ask of you,
If it be pleasing to your high dignity.

King: Madam, tell me your desire.
What boon do you desire from me?

Queen: Now sovereign, worshipful in every way,
I wish to go with you,
To be made a Christian woman;   1700
Gracious lord, I pray it may be so.

King: Alas, because of the irrationality of women's minds,
Mishaps may occur.
Why do you want it? And you are with child.

Queen: My sovereign I will be inconsolable,
Unless you consider what it is I crave,
For all the love you have ever had for me,
Do not leave me behind!

King: Wife, since you insist on having this boon,
There is nothing more I can say.
Now, Jesus be our guide, who is divine justice,
As well as this blessed woman, Mary Magdalene.

Mary: Since you have consented to do this deed,
I will give you God's blessing.
He shall save you from all misfortune.
In the name of the Father, the Son, and the Holy Spirit. Amen.

The Place—The ship enters.

The sailor says,

Sailor: Look ahead, Grobbe my knave,
And tell me what tidings you may,
And if you spy any land.

Boy: I will hasten to climb the rigging.

He climbs.

From what I can ascertain,
By my faith, I see a castle!

Sailor: If we can, set a course,
I know it is a harbor town
That stands on the shore.

They reach the shore.

The king crosses the stage to the ship, and the king says,

King: Good man, where is that ship bound?
Sir, I pray thee tell me.

Sailor: Sir, as for that, it is no secret.
Why do you inquire?

King: Because we have a need, we wish to sail;
We wish to cross the sea.

Sailor: Yes, but I need to by paid, and I fear
That you have little money, since you need to book passage so hastily.
[I think that] you have stolen some man's wife
That you must take out of his land.
Nevertheless, God save me,
Let me see what you can pay me,
Before I decide whether or not I can take you.

King: I will give you ten marks,
If you will take and set us on the cliffs
Of the Holy Land.

They go aboard.

To his crew,

Sailor: Cast off, boy, into the sea;
Hence, we go!

They set sail.

The queen lamenting.

Queen: Lady, help me in my need,
That we not be drown in the sea!
Mary, flower of womanhead,
O blessed lady, do not forget me!

King: My dear wife! Fear not,   1750
But trust in Mary Magdalene
And she will save us from perils;
She will pray to God for us.

Queen: Dear husband, think on me,
And save yourself as long as you may.
For truly it cannot be otherwise;
My heart is very sore this day.
The child that lies in my womb,
Which was honestly conceived—
Alas that there are no midwives to help [deliver me]—
Sorrowful parting splits us,
For truly now, we will part.
Because there are no midwives here in my time of need,
Death is spreading throughout my body.
Now Mary Magdalene, guide my soul,
Into your hands, Lord!

   She dies.

King: Alas, my wife is dead!
Alas, this is a great misfortune!
I fear that my child
Will die for lack of sustenance.
Good Lord grant me grace,
Here is the child of us two
And it is motherless!
Help me, to end my sorrow,
If it be thy will!

Sailor: Bless us, bless us!
What weather is this?

   Storm

Our mast will break asunder!

Boy: Master, I'll bet my ear,
It is because of this dead body that we bear;
Cast her and or else we will sink!

They make ready to cast her body out.

King: Nay, for God's sake, do not do it!
Do not cast her into the sea.
Gentle sirs, for my love—
Yonder is a rock in the west—
Lay her there upon it,
And my child by her.

Sailor: I will assent to that.
As long as she is out of the vessel,
Then we should survive,
Truly I say to you.

They sail to the rock, and the woman and her child are laid there.

King: Lie here, wife and child by thee.
Blessed Magdalene be her guide!
With weeping tears, and with good reason,*   *as circumstances demand
I kiss you both in this hour.
Now will I pray to Mary mild,
Here, to be their guide.

They row to the rock.

The sailor says,

Sailor: Pay now, sir, and go onto the land,
For if I understand correctly, this is the port [you wished to reach].
Put my pay in my hand,   1800
And quickly leave me.

King: I grant that, sir, so God save me.

Pays him.

Here is the price agreed upon;
Quickly thou shall have it
And a mark more than you are due.
And you, page, for your obedience,
Beside what you are owed, I give you
A mark more than your wages.

Sailor: Now, He that has made both day and night,
Speed you rightly on your way,
And give you good passage!

The King of Marseilles travels to Jerusalem where he encounters Peter preaching.

Peter: Now all creatures on the earth,
They are Christ's creatures,
Beholden to worship Jesus
And to never transgress against Him.

King: Sir, faithfully I beseech you this day,
[Whether you know] where I might find Peter the apostle.

Peter: Without delay, sir. It is I.
Tell me why you ask.

King: Sir, I will tell you the truth,
And tell you my reason quickly.
There is a woman named Mary Magdalene,
That has compelled me to come from Marseilles.
I believe there is no guile in that woman.
And she compelled me to make this pilgrimage.
I will tell you more, she said that you
Would christen me and deliver me from woe and harm.

Peter: Blessed be the time that grace befell you,
And if you keep your belief* according to my teaching   *faith
And forever forsake the fiend Satan,
You shall have the commandments of God in your keeping!

King: Truly, I believe in the Father of all creation,
And in the Son, Jesus Christ,
Also in the Holy Ghost, who brings grace to us.
I believe in Christ's death and his resurrection.

Peter: Sir, then what do you ask?

King: For the love of God, holy father, baptism [I seek].
To save me in every way
From the fiend's bondage.

They go to the place of baptism.

Peter: In the name of the Trinity
With this water I baptize you,
That you may stand strong
Against the fiend.

Then he sprinkles him with water.

King: Holy father, my heart will suffer,
If you do not explain the meaning of God's commandments!

Peter: Sir, daily you will study hard
Until you have spiritual enlightenment.
You will dwell with me to increase your understanding,
And with delight go visit the stations,[120]
From Nazareth and Bethlehem and the rest,   1850
And by seeing them, your faith will be strengthened.

The King of Marseilles leaves Peter and returns after a brief time.

King: Now, holy father, precious and dear,
You know my intent.
It has been two full years,
Since I came to you from over the sea
To become Christ's servant and yours
And to fulfill his commandment.
Now I will return home to my country.
Your pure blessing grant us;
That, I faithfully desire.

Peter: Now in the name of Jesus
Go with the Father and the Holy Spirit;
May God keep and protect you!

The king crosses the stage to the ship, and he says,

King: Come near and stop, shipman!

Boy: Sir, yonder is one who called.

Sailor: Aye, sir, I know you of old.
By my truth, you are welcome here.

King: Now gentle mariner, I pray thee,
Whatever I must pay,
Help me pass over the sea,
As quickly as you can.

Sailor: Truly, we are at you service.
Your request will be gladly granted.

---

120 The stations of the cross, portraying Christ's passion and resurrection—can also refer to holy places
visited in their order of occurrence in Christ's life on pilgrimage to Jerusalem.

Don't worry about payment,
Come aboard, in God's name.

The king boards.

Grobbe, boy, the wind is in the north-west;
Quickly turn the sail about!
Hastily raise the sail,
As well as you can!

The ship comes round about the place.

King: Master of the ship, look out there!
I think I spy the rock [where we left my wife].
Gentle master, guide us thither.
I shall pay you.

Sailor: In faith, it is the same rock
That your wife lies upon.
You shall be there quickly,
Truly, indeed.

King: O thou mighty Lord of heaven's domain
Yonder is the baby of my blood,
Preserved and kept from harm!
Blessed by the Lord that succors you!

He lands.

And my wife lies here, fair and undefiled by death!
Fair and clear is her countenance!
Good Lord, you strengthen us with your grace.
You reignite my wife's life!
Blessed be that pure virgin:*[121]   *Mary Magdalene
From grievous sleep* she begins to awaken!   *death
The Son of Grace shines upon us!
Now blessed be God, I see my wife alive!

Queen: O virgin who brought us our salvation,   1900
Pure and chaste, and of noble kinship!
O almighty maiden, our soul's comfort.
O demure Magdalene, my body's sustenance!
Thou had embraced us, protecting us from corruption,

---

121 Mary Magdalene is considered a pure virgin after her repentance and Christ's forgiveness.

And led me with my lord into the Holy Land. [122]
I am baptized, as are you [husband], by Mary's guidance,
And by St. Peter's holy hand.
I saw the blessed cross on which Christ shed his precious blood;
I also saw his blessed sepulcher;
Therefore, good husband, be of good cheer,
For I have visited the stations too.

King: With joyous heart, I thank Jesus
That now I have both my wife and child.
I thank Mary Magdalene and Our Lady Mary,
And ever shall, indeed.

They go aboard, and then they row away from the rock, and the sailor says,

Sailor: Now you are past all peril;
Here is the land of Marseilles!
Now, sir, I pray you
Disembark, when you are ready.

King: Praise God, gentle mariner!
Here is ten pounds of gold coins,
And may God save you and your friends
Both far and near from woe and harm!

They land. The ship leaves the place.

Mary Magdalene says, preaching, as the King and Queen of Marseilles and their son, the prince, approach:

Mary: O dear friends, be constant in heart,
And think on how dear Christ has saved you!
Nothing is impossible for God;
Think how He created all things out of nothing.
Though you may at sometime fall into poverty,[123]
Yet feel the spiritual love both night and day;
For they are blessed that are so afflicted.
For, poverty is God's home.
God blesses all that are meek and good.
And He blesses all those that weep for sinners.
They are blessed that are hungry and that thirst, give them food;
They are blessed that are merciful toward wretched men;
They are blessed that destroy sin.

---

122 In addition to saving mother and child, another miracle—transporting the Queen to the Holy Land
     for her baptism and edification—is attributed to Mary Magdalene.
123 Based on the *Beatitudes*, Matthew 5:1-12.

These are called the children of life,
By He who died on the cross
Who brought bliss to both you and me. Amen.

The king and queen kneel down. The king says,

King: Hail Mary! Our Lord is with thee.[124]
Health and spiritual sustenance for our souls!
Hail, tabernacle of the blessed Trinity!
Hail, comforter, succoring man and wife.

Queen: Hail, thou, alone, chosen and chaste of women!
It is beyond my wit to tell of thy nobleness!
You brought relief to me and my child on the stone rock,
And also saved us with thy great holiness.

Mary: Welcome home, king and queen both!
Welcome home, young prince and heir!
Welcome home to your rightful heritage,[125] doubtless,   1950
And to all your people who have come to greet you!
Now you have become God's own knight;
You sought salve for your soul's health
In the Holy Lands where the Holy Ghost resides,
And have driven away all the fiend's deceits,
And now you have knowledge of the doctrine,
The true way to obtain grace.
Now I bestow your goods and property upon you once again;
I trust I have governed over all as would please you.
Now will I go forth and labor for God,
To make myself more worthy of heaven.

King: O blessed Mary, help us obtain
Greater grace, have pity on us [and do not leave].

Queen: Why depart from us, why venture forth?
O blessed lady, do not so impoverish our souls!

Mary: I will always remember you and yours
And keep you in my daily prayers,
So that you be delivered from all iniquity
And live in peace and quiet.

---

124 Echoes the *Hail Mary* of the Annunciation.
125 Mary recognizes and proclaims the prince is the legitimate successor to the King of Marseilles.

King: Now, then, grant us your pure blessing.

Mary: May the blessing of God fill you completely!
May He who lives and reigns without end bless you!

Mary goes into the wilderness, and the king says,

King: We may sigh and also weep,
That we have lost this noble lady
Who has been our guide and governor!
It brings care and woe to my heart.

Queen: Thinking upon her, that sweet galingale,*   *a herb
Departing from us, I turn pale.
No joy or delight remains for me,
Now that she is gone from our presence.

King: I am not happy about her going,
But I must apply myself to governing my lands.
Like St. Peter bade me,
I will erect churches in cities,
And whoever disputes our faith,
I will punish and persecute those people.
Mohammed and his laws I defy.
Mohammed's pride will be profaned by my love [of Jesus]
For I commit myself wholly to Jesus.

Mary Magdalene in the Wilderness

Mary in the wilderness

Mary: In this desert I will dwell,
To preserve my soul from sin.
I will dwell here in humility,
And patiently devote myself to the Lord.
I will devote myself to charity,
And live in abstinence, all the days of my life.
My conscience directs me so,
And why should I quarrel with my conscience?
And furthermore, I will live in charity
In reverence to Our Blessed Lady,

I will be extremely generous, to strengthen my soul.   2000
I will abstain from all worldly food,
[Living] only by the food the comes from heaven,
The spiritual sustenance sent from God.

Christ in the heavens hears Mary's prayer and calls to his angels.

Jesus: The sweetest of prayers was sent unto me
From my well-beloved friend [who is] always constant [in her love].
She shall be fed with spiritual food.
Angels! Into the clouds raise her up;
There feed her with manna to sustain her[126]—
Let her receive this amid the joy of angels.
Bid her to rejoice with these heavenly companions,
For the fiend's trickery shall never deceive her.

Angel 1: O Thou sweet-smelling rose born of a virgin!
O Thou precious palm of victory!
O Thou hosanna, angel's song!
O precious gem born of Our Lady!
Lord, thy commandment we humbly obey.
We will descend into the wilderness
To thy servant that You have granted bliss;
We angels all devoutly obey.

Two angles descend into the wilderness, and two others bearing the obley, mass bread, openly appearing aloft in the clouds. The two beneath shall lift Mary, and she shall receive the obley and then go again into the wilderness.

Angel 2: Mary, God greets thee with heavenly effusions!
He has sent thee grace with heavenly signs;
Thou shall be honored with joy and reverence,
And raised above all other virgins in heaven!
Thou hast dwelt here among thorns,
God will send miraculous food to thee.
Thou shall be received into the clouds
To receive spiritual food for thy salvation.

Mary: Your will be done in heaven and on earth!
Now I am full of joy and bliss.
Pray and praise that blessed birth!
I am ready at his blessed will.

---

126 Many hagiographies contain stories of saints sustained solely by manna delivered from heaven.

She is embraced by the angels, who sing a reverent song, as she is raised into the clouds and fed the obley.

Mary has been taken into the clouds;[127] *the heavens rejoice, and the angels praise the Son of God. Mary says,*

Mary: O thou Lord of lords of high dominion!
In heaven and earth thy name is worshipped.
Thou hath kept me from hunger and anguish!
O glorious Lord, in Thee is no dishonesty or villainy.
If I were not to serve my Lord, I should be blamed,
He who filled me with the greatest joy,
Has fed me with food most dear,
And given me joy and delight amid the melody of angels!

She returns to the wilderness.

A holy priest in the same wilderness speaks, saying:

Priest: O Lord of lords, what may this be?
What great mysteries appeared from heaven,
With angles bright as lightning
[Bringing] great mirth and heavenly melody?
Lord Jesus, by the seven names,
Grant me thy grace to see that person.

Here he goes into the wilderness and sees Mary at her devotion.

Priest: Hail creature, Christ's delight!
Hail thee, sweeter than sugar or galingale!
Mary is thy name from what the angels say.
Beloved are you to God for your perfection.
You were shown the joy of the heavenly Jerusalem,   2050
The likes of which I have not seen in thirty years or more.
Therefore, I know well thou are a saint.[128]
I will pray to you earnestly to show me a revelation of your Lord.

Mary: By the grace of my Lord Jesus.
For thirty winters, this has been my cell,
And thrice daily have I been raised up,
With more joy than any tongue can tell.
No creature has come to this place where I dwell
At any time, day or night,

---

127 Echoes the assumption of the Virgin Mary and invoked by use of the Latin word, **assumpta**.

128 The priest witnessing of the miracle of Mary's ascension serves to establish her sainthood, which is one of the intentions of the play. His presence is also necessary so that she can receive Last Rites.

Except for God's angels bright.
But thou art welcome into my sight,
If thou live in a righteous way;
I delight in thinking
Thou are a man of religious orders.

Priest: In Christ's law I am ordained, a priest
Assisted by angels at the mass,
I consecrate the body of our Lord Jesus Christ
And by that manna I live by the righteous path.

Mary: Now I rejoice in your holiness!
The time has come that I shall ascend.

Priest: I commend myself to you with all humility.
I intend to go to my cell.[129]

    The priest goes to his cell.

    In heaven, Jesus says,

Jesus: Now shall Mary have possession of the crown
That is her rightful inheritance to bear;
She shall be brought into everlasting salvation,
To dwell in joy; she who is without rival.
Now, angels, quickly go there!
Appear now in the priest's cell,
Tell him to give my body in the form of bread,
Tell him to administer the Eucharist* to her.   *as part of the Last Rites
Angel 1: O blessed Lord, we are ready
To obey and deliver your message.

Angel 2: I will go to her and tell her.

    The two angels go to Mary and to the priest.

    The angels say to the priest,

Angels: Sir priest, from heaven, God commands
That you quickly go administer the Eucharist to his servant.
We shall assist you
And bear light before his worthy body.

---

129 Priests and monks rooms were often called cells.

Priest: Angels, with all humility
I will dress myself in a vestment;* *priest's attire while performing Church duties
I will go there right away
To administer the Eucharist.

The second angel goes to Mary in the wilderness and says,

Angel 2: Mary be glad and of strong heart;
Ready yourself to receive the palm of great victory,
This day you shall ascend with angels' song;
Your soul shall depart from your body.

Mary: Ah, good Lord, I thank thee without any reservation!
This day I am firmly grounded in goodness.
My heart stops and my body dies.   2100
With perfect devotion, I thank thee, Lord.

The angels appear, and then the priest comes with the Eucharist.

Priest: Thou blessed woman, practiced in meekness,
I have brought the bread of life into you sight,
To succor you from all distress
And to bring thy soul into the everlasting light.

Mary: O thou mighty Lord of high majesty,
At this time, You have determined that
I receive this celestial bread
To thereby illuminate my soul.

She receives it.

I thank thee, Lord of ardent love!
Now I well know that I have nothing to fear.
Lord, let me see thy joys above!
I commend my spirit into your bliss.
Lord, open thy blessed gates!
At this time, I fervently kiss the earth.
Into your hands, Lord—
Lord, guide me with your grace!
I commend my spirit. You have redeemed me,[130]
Lord God of truth.

She ascends with the angels.

---

130 Echoes Christ's last words to his Father on the cross.

Angel 1: Now we receive this soul into heaven to dwell among us,
As is only right and just.

Angel 2: In bliss without end,
Now let us sing a merry song.

They rejoice in heaven.

Remaining below, the priest says,

Priest: O good God, great is thy grace!
O Jesus, Jesus, blessed is thy name!
Mary, Mary, great is thy joy,
In heaven's bliss find happiness and delight!
Thy body will I inter;
I will go to the bishop of the city
And ask permission to bury Mary's body
With all reverence and solemnity.

The priest addresses the audience in an epilogue.

Sirs, here [we] end the narration that we have performed
In your presence, with this message:
All-mighty God, most of magnificence,
Bring You his bliss so bright
In the presence of Christ the King.
Now, friends, thus ends this play.
May God give bliss to those that have been here!
Now, clerics with voices clear,
We praise you, God; let us sing.

Here ends the original [play] of Saint Mary Magdalene.

Scribal postscript:

If anything be amiss,
Blame my lack of understanding and do not think it intended.
Please, readers be my friends;
If there is anything erroneous, please correct it.

Bibliography

Amodio, Mark. "Oral Poetics in Post-Conquest England." *Oral Poetics in Middle English Poetry*. Edited by Mark Amodio. New York: Garland, 1994, 1-17.

Bennett, William. "Communication and Excommunication in the '*N-Town* Conception of Mary." *Assays: Critical Approaches to Medieval and Renaissance Texts* 8 (1995), 119-140.

Bynum, Caroline. *Holy Feast and Holy Fast: The Religious Significance of Food to Medieval Women*. Berkeley: University of California Press, 1987.

------. *Jesus As Mother: Studies In The Spirituality Of The High Middle Ages*. Berkeley: University of California Press, 1982.

Carlson, Cindy. "Mary's Obedience and Power in the 'Trial of Mary and Joseph.'" *Comparative Drama* 29(1995), 348-62.

Clopper, Lawrence. *Drama, Play, And Game: English Festive Culture In The Medieval And Early Modern Period*. Chicago: University of Chicago Press, 2001.

Coletti, Theresa. *Mary Magdalene And The Drama Of Saints: Theater, Gender, And Religion In Late Medieval England*. Philadelphia: University of Pennsylvania Press, 2004.

-------. "Purity and Danger The Paradox of Mary's Body and the En-Gendering of the Infancy Narrative in the English Mystery Cycles." *Feminist Approaches to the Body in Medieval Literature*. Edited by Lomperis, Linda and Sarah Stanbury. Philadelphia: University of Pennsylvania, 1993, 65-95.

Coon, Lynda, Katherine Haldane, and Elisabeth Sommer, editors. *That Gentle Strength: Historical Perspectives on Women and Christianity*. Charlottesville: University of Virginia Press, 1990.

Davidson, Clifford. "*The Digby Mary Magdalene* and the Magdalene Cult of the Middle Ages." *Annuale Mediaevale*, 13 (1972): 70-87.

The Digby Mary Magdalene in *Medieval Drama*. Compiled by David Bevington. Boston: Houghton Mifflin, 1975.

Early Christian Writings. Compiled and edited by Kirby, Peter. (Last updated, 2014). Http://www.earlychristianwritings.com.

Ehrman, Bart. *Lost Christianities*. New York: Oxford, 2003.

-------. *Misquoting Jesus*. San Francisco: Harper, 2005.

Fitzhenry, William. "The *N-Town Plays* and the Politics of Metatheater." *Studies in Philology* 100.1 (2003): 22-43.

Foley, John Miles. "The Implications of Oral Tradition." In Oral Tradition in the Middle Ages. Edited by W.F. H. Nicolaisen. Binghamton: Medieval and Renaissance Texts and Studies, 1995, 31-57.

Gibson, Gail McMurray. *Theater of Devotion: East Anglian Drama and Society in the Late Middle Ages*. Chicago: University of Chicago Press, 1989.

Granger, Penny. *The N-Town Play: Drama and Liturgy in Medieval East Anglia.* London: Brewer, 2009.

Head, Thomas. "The Religion of the Femmelettes: Ideals and Experience Among Women in Fifteenth- and Sixteenth-Century France." In *That Gentle Strength: Historical Perspectives on Women and Christianity.* Edited by Lynda Coon, Katherine Haldane, and Elisabeth Sommer. Charlottesville, University of Virginia Press, 1990, 149-75.

--------. *Soldiers of Christ: Saints and Saints' Lives from Late Antiquity and the Early Middle Ages.* Edited by Thomas Noble and Thomas Head. University Park: Pennsylvania State University Press, 1994.

Hill-Vásquez, Heather. *Sacred players: The Politics of Response in the Middle English Religious Drama.* Washington, D.C.: Catholic University of America Press, 2007.

Irvine, Martin. "Medieval Textuality and the Archaeology of Textual Cultural." *Speaking Two Languages: Traditional Disciplines and Contemporary Theory in Medieval Studies.* Edited by Allen Frantzen. Albany: State University of New York Press, (1991) 181-206.

Jacobus de Voragine. *Aurea Legenda (The Golden Legend),* 1275. Translated by William Caxton (1483). http://legacy.fordham.edu/halsall/basis/goldenlegend/GoldenLegend-Volume4.asp#Mary%20Magdalene.

Jansen, Katherine L. *The Making of the Magdalen: Preaching and Popular Devotion in the Later Middle Ages.* Princeton: Princeton University Press, 2001.

King, Karen. *The Gospel of Mary of Magdala: Jesus and the First Woman Apostle.* Santa Rosa: Polebridge, 2003.

Kinservik, Matthew. "The Struggle over Mary's Body: Theological and Dramatic Resolution in the 'N-Town Assumption Play.'" *Journal of English and Germanic Philology* 95. 2 (1996): 190-203.

Lord, Albert. "Oral Composition and 'Oral Residue' in the Middle Ages." *Oral Tradition in the Middle Ages.* Edited by W.F. H. Nicolaisen. Binghamton: Medieval and Renaissance Texts and Studies, 1995: 7-29.

Ludus Coventiae in English Mystery Plays. Edited by Peter Happé. (Middlesex: Penguin) 1975.

"Mary Magdalene." *Early South English Legendary.* April 30, 2009. Http://www.lib.rochester.edu/camelot/teams/14sr/htm.

The Mary Play from the N-Town Manuscript. Edited by Peter Meredith. London: Longman, 1987.

Metzger, Bruce and Bart Ehrman. *The Text of the New Testament: Its Transmission, Corruption and Restoration.* Fourth Edition. New York: Oxford, 2005.

The N-Town play: Cotton MS Vespasian D.8. Edited by Stephen Spector. Oxford: Early English Text Society, 1991.

Moll, Richard. "Staging Disorder: Charivari in the *N-Town Cycle.*" *Comparative Drama* 35 (2001): 145-61.

N-Town Plays in TEAMS Middle English Texts. Edited by Douglas Sugano. Kalamazoo: Western Michigan University Press, 2007.

The Nag Hammadi Scriptures. Edited by Marvin Meyer. New York: Harper One, 2007.

The New Advent Catholic Encyclopedia. http://newadvent.org/cathen/

Newman, Barbara. *From Virile Woman to WomanChrist: Studies in Medieval Religion and Literature*. Philadelphia: University of Pennsylvania Press, 1995.

Pagels, Elaine. *The Gnostic Gospels*. New York: Vintage, 1989.

Renoir, Alain. "Oral-Formulaic Rhetoric, An Approach to Image and Message in Medieval Poetry." In *Medieval Texts and Contemporary Readers*. Edited by Laurie Finke and Martin Shichtman. Ithaca: Cornell, 1987: 234-53.

----------. "Oral Theme and Written Texts." *Neuphilologische Mitteilungen* 77(1976): 337-46.

Robertson, Elizabeth. *Early English Devotional Prose and the Female Audience*. Knoxville: University of Tennessee Press, 1990.

Shahar, Shulamith. *The Fourth Estate: A History of Women in the Middle Ages*. New York: Routledge, 2003.

Stark, Rodney. *The Rise of Christianity*. San Francisco: Harper, 1996.

Stevenson, Jill. *Performance, Cognitive Theory, and Devotional Culture: Sensual Piety in late Medieval York*. New York: Palgrave Macmillan, 2010.

Vauchez, André. *The Laity in the Middle Ages: Religious Beliefs and Devotional Practices*. Translated by Margery Schneider. Notre Dame: Notre Dame Press, 1993.

Woolf, Rosemary. *The English Mystery Plays*. Berkeley: University of California Press, 1972.